REPORT

Future Challenges for the Arab World

The Implications of Demographic and Economic Trends

Keith Crane, Steven Simon, Jeffrey Martini

Prepared for the United States Air Force

Approved for public release; distribution unlimited

RAND PROJECT AIR FORCE

The research described in this report was sponsored by the United States Air Force under Contract FA7014-06-C-0001. Further information may be obtained from the Strategic Planning Division, Directorate of Plans, Hq USAF.

Library of Congress Control Number: 2011927725

ISBN: 978-0-8330-5100-4

The RAND Corporation is a nonprofit institution that helps improve policy and decisionmaking through research and analysis. RAND's publications do not necessarily reflect the opinions of its research clients and sponsors.

RAND® is a registered trademark.

© Copyright 2011 RAND Corporation

Permission is given to duplicate this document for personal use only, as long as it is unaltered and complete. Copies may not be duplicated for commercial purposes. Unauthorized posting of RAND documents to a non-RAND website is prohibited. RAND documents are protected under copyright law. For information on reprint and linking permissions, please visit the RAND permissions page (http://www.rand.org/publications/ permissions.html).

Published 2011 by the RAND Corporation
1776 Main Street, P.O. Box 2138, Santa Monica, CA 90407-2138
1200 South Hayes Street, Arlington, VA 22202-5050
4570 Fifth Avenue, Suite 600, Pittsburgh, PA 15213-2665
RAND URL: http://www.rand.org/
To order RAND documents or to obtain additional information, contact
Distribution Services: Telephone: (310) 451-7002;
Fax: (310) 451-6915; Email: order@rand.org

Preface

This report describes an assessment of likely demographic and economic trends in the Arab world through 2020. The report is designed to provide U.S. Air Force (USAF) and Department of Defense analysts a more-informed platform on which to build defense planning and U.S. policy. We have attempted to focus on trends that are likely to persist and assess how these trends are likely to affect U.S. interests, regardless of how the war in Iraq or the conflict between Israelis and Palestinians are resolved.

The research reported here was sponsored by the Director for Operational Plans and Joint Matters (AF/A5X), Headquarters U.S. Air Force. The original work was conducted within the Strategy and Doctrine Program of RAND Project AIR FORCE as part of a fiscal year 2004 study, "USAF Posture in the Greater Middle East." It has been extensively revised and updated to 2009.

Related RAND Project AIR FORCE publications include the following:

- *Pakistan: Can the United States Secure an Insecure State?* C. Christine Fair, Keith Crane, Christopher S. Chivvis, Samir Puri, and Michael Spirtas (MG-910-AF, 2010)
- *The Iraq Effect: The Middle East After the Iraq War*, Frederic Wehrey, Dalia Dassa Kaye, Jessica Watkins, Jeffrey Martini, and Robert A. Guffey (MG-892-AF, 2010)
- *Troubled Partnership: U.S.-Turkish Relations in an Era of Global Geopolitical Change*, F. Stephen Larrabee (MG-899-AF, 2010)
- *Radical Islam in East Africa*, Angel Rabasa (MG-782-AF, 2009)
- *Future U.S. Security Relationships with Iraq and Afghanistan: U.S. Air Force Roles*, David E. Thaler, Theodore W. Karasik, Dalia Dassa Kaye, Jennifer D. P. Moroney, Frederic Wehrey, Obaid Younossi, Farhana Ali, and Robert A. Guffey (MG-681-AF, 2008).

RAND Project AIR FORCE

RAND Project AIR FORCE (PAF), a division of the RAND Corporation, is the U.S. Air Force's federally funded research and development center for studies and analyses. PAF provides the Air Force with independent analyses of policy alternatives affecting the development, employment, combat readiness, and support of current and future aerospace forces. Research is conducted in four programs: Force Modernization and Employment; Manpower, Personnel, and Training; Resource Management; and Strategy and Doctrine.

Additional information about PAF is available on our website:
http://www.rand.org/paf

Contents

Figures and Table

Figures

Table

Summary

The purpose of this technical report is to help USAF and Department of Defense analysts assess likely demographic and economic challenges in the Arab world through 2020, a region of primary concern for U.S. security and foreign policies. The report is designed to provide a more-informed platform on which to build U.S. defense planning and policy. The report references conflicts in the region but focuses on longer-term, region-wide trends that are likely to affect U.S. interests no matter how events in Iraq or between Israel and Palestine unfold.

The Pressure of People

In terms of population, the Arab world remains the second-most rapidly growing region in the world after sub-Saharan Africa. But even though cultural factors have contributed to higher fertility rates than in countries with similar standards of living, population growth rates have fallen sharply everywhere but in the West Bank and Gaza. Population growth rates are projected to continue to decline as the region experiences the same downward pressures on fertility that have resulted in slower population growth in East and South Asia and Latin America.

Because of the large increases in population in the 1980s and 1990s, the numbers of young people entering the labor markets of these countries have been rising rapidly and will continue to do so for the next two decades, adding to the difficulties young people currently face in finding employment.

Due to variations in birth rates and migration, religious diversity in the Arab world is declining. The dwindling of non-Muslim religious communities reduces the number of citizens making the argument for a secular state. Secular influences in the form of more female participation in education and the labor force and through movies and television now have a greater impact on these societies than religious diversity.

Economic Performance of the Energy Rich

For the foreseeable future, the world will continue to depend on oil pumped from the Arab region, especially the Persian Gulf. The region will continue to account for a third of global production in 2020. Even if rates of depletion are higher than previously estimated and production costs in the Persian Gulf double or triple their current levels of just a few dollars per barrel, the Gulf states will remain the world's lowest-cost producers. They will hold more than half of global reserves.

Despite their oil riches, the "energy-rich" countries in the region fell on hard times after the oil boom of the 1970s ended. In most countries in the Gulf, per capita gross domestic product (GDP) in constant-dollar terms is still below previous peaks. The primary reason for the poor economic performance of these larger countries has been declines in factor productivity. These declines have been due to poor investment decisions and microeconomic policies, especially price subsidies and bureaucratic barriers to the entry of new firms into markets.

Economic output in the energy rich, especially for the smaller Gulf states, will continue to be closely linked to oil output and prices. However, oil and gas exports will serve more as a foundation than a driver of growth. Only in Iraq and Qatar are increases in oil production likely to exceed population growth through 2020. Although energy will continue to provide a ready source of revenues to governments, the key to increasing per capita incomes will be increasing factor productivity.

To increase factor productivity,[1] these countries need to reduce price distortions by cutting producer and, to the extent politically feasible, consumer price subsidies. Barriers to trade and foreign investment need to be reduced, especially in Algeria and Libya. Continued expansion and integration of the Gulf Cooperation Council (GCC) would do much to increase competition and improve factor productivity in those countries. Privatization of non–energy-sector assets has improved efficiency and generated more-rapid growth in revenues and output of formerly state-owned enterprises in those Arab countries that have braved this step. A more-aggressive approach to privatization would generate additional benefits in terms of accelerated growth in factor productivity.

How likely are the governments of the energy-rich countries to adopt policies that would foster more-efficient use of resources? Going forward, we expect the GCC countries to continue to push ahead with economic liberalization, regional integration, and privatization. If oil prices continue to stay substantially higher than their average levels of the 1990s, the citizens of the smaller countries should continue to enjoy high levels of income and continued growth. Algeria, Iraq, Libya, and, to a lesser extent, Saudi Arabia are poorer, have larger populations, and, as can be seen by recent events in Libya, are more vulnerable to political unrest.

None of the energy rich has successfully addressed the issue of state employment. These governments will need to devise incentives to encourage new entrants to the labor force to seek jobs outside of government. Modest shifts in expectations have taken place in some of these countries, as jobs in private finance and some service industries have become socially acceptable, but the government overwhelmingly remains the preferred employer. In light of the political difficulties, we do not expect these states to cut employment of nationals in overstaffed state bureaucracies or state-controlled companies.

Prospects for Growth in the Energy Poor

Improvements in economic policies from unifying exchange rates, reducing tariffs and other barriers to trade, and privatization have contributed to more-rapid growth in all but one of the "energy poor" over the past two decades than was the case in the 1980s. In most instances, higher oil prices have also helped the energy poor as demand for foreign labor has risen in the

---

[1] The amount of additional output that inputs of capital and labor are able to generate.

Gulf, leading to increased remittances and, in the case of Egypt and Syria, bumping up the value of their own modest exports of oil and natural gas.

Like most of the energy rich, the energy poor suffered from the global recession, but, for the most part, their economies are projected to continue to grow. Exports, remittances, and incomes from tourism are falling, but lower commodity prices, especially for food and petroleum products, have eased pressures on the poor. With some luck, these countries could soon see a return to growth rates of the recent past. If growth recovers to the rates of the recent past, the energy poor will enjoy appreciable increases in per capita incomes through 2020, with per capita GDP rising by 3.0 percent per annum in the case of Egypt and 4.5 percent in the case of Jordan, as solid growth in GDP is accompanied by slower rates of growth in population.

How likely is it that these rates of economic growth will resume? Egypt, Jordan, Morocco, and Tunisia have made significant moves toward liberalizing their economies, especially trade, over the past decade. Free-trade agreements with the European Union (EU) and the United States have helped spur this development. Some progress has been made on liberalizing controlled prices on refined oil products and food and better targeting food and other subsidies. A number of formerly state-owned companies have been privatized. The energy poor have also attempted to make their local business climates more hospitable for private entrepreneurs.

To make further progress in reducing barriers to entry for new businesses and to foster private-sector job creation, the governments will need to markedly improve the efficiency of their bureaucracies and social welfare systems. Making the bureaucracy more efficient will not only entail streamlining procedures but also involve cutting staffs and linking rewards to performance. Because of the entrenched opposition of the bureaucracy, implementing these changes will be difficult. In addition, despite some reforms, these governments preserve expensive, often dysfunctional systems of subsidies. Making further changes in these systems is likely to be politically difficult.

Under conditions of a return to the growth rates of the recent past, the outlook for growth in employment and wages is positive. Rates of unemployment have dropped sharply in Algeria, Morocco, and a few other Arab countries in recent years. Privatization of state-owned enterprises has increased labor productivity and, counterintuitively, employment by lowering the cost of business services and making the labor market more flexible. But governments in the region still impose strictures on firing, hiring, and minimum wages that have discouraged businesses from hiring and entrepreneurs from investing. Additional measures to improve labor market flexibility and a shift in social acceptance of female participation in the labor force are likely to increase employment and accelerate growth. In all but Yemen, growth rates should be rapid enough that real wages will rise along with employment.

Institutional reform will not be the sole factor determining economic growth. For most of the energy poor, security—internal and external—will remain a key determinant of growth. As shown by the recent events in the region, countries suffer economically from conflict, either domestic or from spillover effects from neighboring states. Countries suffer substantial economic losses from unrest and conflict, especially from falloffs in tourism revenues. If security remains a major problem, economic growth will suffer. For example, Egypt and Tunisia experienced falloffs in tourism revenues from their unrest.

Policy Implications

In the light of these trends and challenges, we make the following policy recommendations:

- Although fertility rates and population growth rates have been declining, the population of the Arab world is still growing more rapidly than in other parts of the world. Increasing populations are straining water resources, public services, and infrastructure. However, fertility rates are not uniform: Some Arab countries have much higher fertility rates than others. Slower rates of population growth would ease pressures on water supplies and on governments to provide more public services, especially in countries with rapid rates of population growth. Over time, slower rates of population growth would permit Arab governments to shift from focusing on quantity to improving quality. U.S. assistance programs can help ease these pressures by continuing to support family-planning initiatives across the region, especially in countries that have higher fertility rates. More U.S. funding to train local staff to conduct outreach and to make contraceptives more widely available would be valuable, as would more indirectly supporting female education.

- Policy toward Arab migrants resident—or attempting to reside—in the United States and Europe will be an increasingly important factor influencing their host-government policies toward the Arab and Muslim worlds. At a minimum, policymakers should recognize that Arab and Muslim communities abroad are now a critical part of the regional equation and will provide an increasingly important window into political futures in the region itself. They are a valuable point of engagement, from counterterrorism to political and economic reform. The special prominence of Muslim communities and political networks in Europe, and their close connection to developments in North Africa and elsewhere, also means that there is a strong argument to be made for transatlantic coordination in this as in many other facets of regional strategy.

- Procedures to provide tourist, student, and business visas to the United States can have major effects on U.S. influence in the region. The large numbers of Arabs who have studied, lived, and worked in the United States have been a major source of U.S. influence in the region. The sharp decline in the numbers of Arab students studying in the United States following September 11 because of more-stringent visa regulations is detrimental to U.S. interests. The U.S. government should carefully review current procedures to ensure both that they prevent the entry of individuals seeking to harm the United States but also that Arabs seeking to visit the United States to study, visit, or conduct business are able to visit this country and are treated with respect when doing so.

- U.S. development agencies should continue to support family-planning initiatives across the region. This can be accomplished by training local staff in outreach and making contraceptives more widely available and indirectly by supporting female education. Given the sensitivities of family planning among some religious conservatives in the region, the United States should take pains to build off of local initiatives and, to the extent possible, keep local organizations as the "face" of these programs and the primary interface with communities.

- Outside of discussions with governments of major oil exporters concerning broader roles for foreign, including U.S., companies in their energy industries, we believe that the U.S. government should relegate discussions about oil output and markets to low levels. In our view, high-level discussions about oil output and prices muddy other U.S. messages concerning economic policies. These discussions might also give the governments of the energy rich an exaggerated sense of the importance of lower-cost oil for the long-term health of the U.S. economy. A focus on preventing increases in oil prices runs counter to the U.S. government's commitment to reduce U.S. emissions of carbon dioxide and other greenhouse gases, undercutting achievement of another major policy goal, the reduction in U.S. consumption of fossil fuels.

- In its role as a board member of both the World Bank and the International Monetary Fund, the United States should strongly support programs and loans that encourage economic liberalization in the region. The United States should work closely with these organizations and channel its economic assistance to encourage these countries to better target subsidies and reduce costs and hurdles facing the private sector. The United States should also negotiate and sign free-trade agreements with friendly countries in the region.

Acknowledgments

We would like to thank three very helpful reviewers: Dalia Dassa Kaye and Krishna Kumar of RAND and Gregory Gause of the University of Vermont. We would also like to thank Andrew Hoehn, Lynn Davis, Jennifer Moroney, David Ochmanek, and Paula Thornhill for supporting this project over a long period, interrupted by a number of fits and starts. Paul Steinberg and Jennifer Miller were instrumental in completing the final publication.

Abbreviations

AF/A5X	Director for Operational Plans and Joint Matters
CIA	Central Intelligence Agency
DoD	U.S. Department of Defense
EIA	Energy Information Administration
EU	European Union
FIS	Front Islamique du Salut, or Islamic Salvation Front
G-20	Group of Twenty
GCC	Gulf Cooperation Council
GDP	gross domestic product
GIA	Groupe Islamique Armé, or Armed Islamic Group
GICM	Groupe Islamique Combattant Marocain, or Moroccan Islamic Combatant Group
ILO	International Labour Organization
MBD	million barrels per day
OECD	Organisation for Economic Co-Operation and Development
OPEC	Organization of the Petroleum Exporting Countries
PAF	Project AIR FORCE
PPP	purchasing power parity
UAE	United Arab Emirates
USAF	U.S. Air Force
WTO	World Trade Organization

CHAPTER ONE

Introduction

Background

In this decade, the Arab world—the Arabic-speaking countries stretching from Morocco to Oman—has replaced Europe and East Asia as the United States' primary security and foreign policy concern. The United States remains heavily engaged in Iraq and is an important third party to two other conflicts in the region: the Israeli-Palestinian quarrel and the turmoil in Lebanon. In addition, the region has been the source of terrorist groups that have perpetrated attacks around the globe, including on the United States. Notwithstanding high-profile attacks in the United States and Europe, these terrorist groups have focused most of their activities on the Arab world: The region has been subject to more terrorist attacks than any other in the world.[1]

Although a number of trends are affecting the region, demographic and economic trends will have a dramatic impact. Demographically speaking, few places in the world are subject to as much pressure from growing numbers of people as the Arab world. Population growth is taxing water supplies, housing, transportation systems, and labor markets. Competition for jobs, especially government jobs, and housing and the poor quality and inadequate provision of public services are prime causes of the deep dissatisfaction with the status quo that marks so many of these societies. The stress these demographic pressures exert—and regional governments' ability to mitigate them—will play a major role in determining the future trajectory of the region.

In terms of their economies, the nations of the Arab world can be categorized into two groups: the "energy rich" and the "energy poor." Of the 18 countries that we cover in this report, 13 of them, particularly those of the Persian Gulf states, are indelibly linked to energy. Of these, we classify nine—Algeria, Bahrain, Iraq, Kuwait, Libya, Oman, Qatar, Saudi Arabia, and the United Arab Emirates (UAE)—as the energy rich, countries for which energy exports constitute half or more of total exports of goods and services, for which energy contributes one-third or more of gross domestic product (GDP), and who have a per capita income at purchasing power parity (PPP) rates of at least $3,200 in 2005 dollars. The second group, the energy-poor countries in this report—Egypt, Jordan, Lebanon, Morocco, Syria, Tunisia, the Palestinian territories, and Yemen—are countries or entities for which economic sectors and exports other than energy play the crucial roles in shaping their economies and that tend to be much poorer than their energy-rich counterparts in the region. Trends in these two groups have very different implications for the region and for U.S. interests in the region.

---

[1] National Counterterrorism Center, *2007 Report on Terrorism*, Washington, D.C., April 30, 2008, pp. 21–22.

Objective and Scope

This report is intended to help U.S. Air Force (USAF) and U.S. Department of Defense (DoD) analysts assess likely demographic and economic trends in the Arab world through 2020 so that defense planning and U.S. policy will have a more-informed platform on which to build. For this report, we define *the Arab world* as Algeria, Bahrain, Egypt, Iraq, Jordan, Kuwait, Lebanon, Libya, Morocco, Oman, the Palestinian territories, Qatar, Saudi Arabia, Syria, Tunisia, the UAE, and Yemen. Even though they are also members of the Arab League, we exclude Comoros, Djibouti, and Somalia, because they are not geographically contiguous with the Arab world and Arabic is not the primary language spoken in these countries. We also excluded Sudan and Mauritania because substantial parts of their populations are better grouped with those in sub-Saharan Africa. Israel and Iran are, of course, not part of the Arab world.

The report also does not directly address postwar Iraq, the Israeli-Palestinian conflict, Lebanon, or the current revolutions. Because they have been covered so extensively elsewhere, we felt we could add little additional value to the analysis of these issues. Rather, we have attempted to focus on demographic and economic trends that are likely to persist across the region and assess how these trends are likely to affect U.S. interests, regardless of how the war in Iraq or the conflict between Israelis and Palestinians are resolved.

Organization of This Document

The report consists of three chapters that investigate the demographic and economic trends in the region and a concluding chapter that draws some policy implications based on the analyses. Like the rest of the world, most Arab countries have entered a period of slower population growth. However, the consequences of past rapid rates of growth in poor, arid countries pose major challenges. In the next chapter, we assess the consequences of past, current, and likely future rates of growth in population for the economies and social stability in these countries, including the implications of divergent rates of growth among the poorer and richer countries of the region. We also assess the implications of different birth rates for the ethnic and religious minorities in the region and how those changes will affect the future political and social landscape.

Chapters Three and Four evaluate economic developments for two sets of countries: the energy rich and the energy poor. Chapters Three and Four follow a similar structures, with the exception that Chapter Three starts with a look at the role of oil and gas in the economies of the energy rich and evaluates the economic implications that likely future trends in oil and gas output and exports would have for these countries. Both chapters then examine trends in economic growth and future prospects, as well as identify those factors and policies that have done the most to affect that growth. They include sections that speculate on likely future trends in economic growth under scenarios assuming better and worse sets of economic policies. The chapters conclude with an assessment of changes in labor markets and the implications of these changes for the economies and societies in the region.

The final chapter discusses the implications of these demographic and economic trends for the future of the Arab world, focusing on policy implications for U.S. national security policymakers.

CHAPTER TWO

Population Growth in the Arab World: The Pressure of People

Few places in the world are subject to as much pressure from growing numbers of people as the Arab world. Population growth is taxing water supplies, housing, transportation systems, and labor markets. Competition for jobs, especially government jobs, and housing and the poor quality and inadequate provision of public services are prime causes of the deep dissatisfaction with the status quo that marks so many of these societies. The stress these demographic pressures exert—and regional governments' ability to mitigate them—will play a major role in determining the future trajectory of the region.

In this chapter, we focus on the demographic pressures and their impacts and assess demographic trends out to 2020, the time frame for this report. In particular, we look at trends in population growth, shifts in population, shifts in the proportion of minorities and ethnic groups in the total population, and shifts in resource constraints across the region. Some of the key findings from that assessment are the following:

- The Arab world remains the second-most rapidly growing region in the world. But even though culture and religion have contributed to relatively high fertility rates, the region is experiencing the same downward trends in fertility and population growth characteristic of Asia and Latin America.
- Population growth rates have fallen sharply everywhere but in the West Bank and Gaza. By 2020, regional population growth rates are projected to fall from 1.7 percent in 2007 to 1.4 percent in 2020; in 2000, the region's population was growing by 2.3 percent per year. By and large, the countries in the region have higher fertility rates and, thus, more-rapid rates of population growth than countries with comparable standards of living elsewhere in the world.
- Because of the large increases in population in the 1980s and 1990s, the numbers of young people entering the labor markets of these countries has been rising rapidly. The labor supply will continue to expand rapidly for the next decade, adding to the difficulties young people face in finding employment that meets their expectations.
- The Arab world is becoming increasingly Muslim. The dwindling of non-Muslim religious communities in the Arab states makes the argument for a secular state that much more difficult to advance. However, secular influences in the form of more female participation in education and the labor force and through movies and television, Western and Arab alike, are contributing to changes in the role of women in society, acceptable social behavior, and differing interpretations of Islam.

We discuss these findings in more detail in the remainder of this chapter.

Demographic Trends in the Arab World

In this section, we examine trends in rates of population growth, fertility, and migration in the Arab world—as well as within Israel and the West Bank and Gaza—and then look at some of the implications of those trends for the region. We conclude with a discussion of how valid those trends seem to be.

Trends in Population Size

When we look at the current population of the Arab world, the actual numbers are not overwhelming: In 2009, the Near East was home to 128 million people, while North Africa had a population of 169 million, for a total of 297 million people (as shown in Figure 2.1). This is just slightly less than the 307 million inhabitants of the United States and substantially less than the 401 million people of Western Europe.

However, as the figure shows, the Arab world has grown very rapidly over the past several decades. In 1950, there were only 67 million people in the region; by 2009, there were nearly four and half times this number. This makes this region the second-fastest growing in the world over that period, lagging only behind sub-Saharan Africa.[1] And in terms of projecting outward, by 2020, the population is expected to have grown to more than five and a half times the 1950 number. Moreover, because of the structure of the region's population—disproportionately young—there will be a significant lag before declining fertility rates will rein in population growth.

Figure 2.1
Population of the Arab World

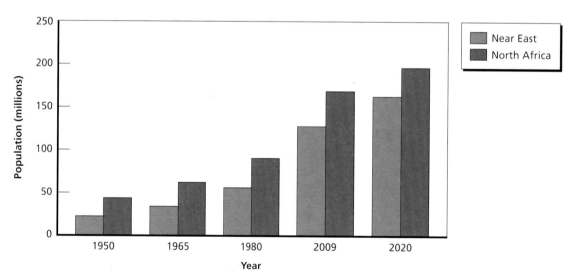

SOURCE: U.S. Census Bureau, *International Data Base*, Washington, D.C., accessed February 8, 2008.
RAND *TR912-2.1*

---

[1]   All population numbers cited in this report are, unless otherwise noted, from the U.S. Census Bureau's *International Data Base*. This online database service provides one of the most-consistent, all-encompassing sources of demographic data and forecasts available.

Trends in Fertility Rates in the Arab World

By and large, the countries in the region have higher fertility rates and, thus, more-rapid rates of population growth than countries with comparable standards of living elsewhere in the world. For example, fertility rates in Saudi Arabia are 3.4 children per woman (Figure 2.2), while, in the Czech Republic and South Korea, countries with almost identical per capita GDPs, rates are 1.4 and 1.3 children per woman, respectively. Kuwait, with a per capita GDP comparable to that of Spain, had a fertility rate of 2.9 children per woman in 2007 compared to 1.3 in Spain. (A rate of 2.1 children roughly serves to replace the current generation.)

While the Persian Gulf countries have the highest fertility rates in the Arab world, North African and Levantine countries are also experiencing higher-than-expected fertility rates given their levels of socioeconomic development. In 2007, fertility rates in Egypt and Morocco ran 2.8 and 2.6 children, respectively. Countries with comparable per capita GDPs at PPP exchange rates, such as Guyana and Sri Lanka, both had fertility rates of 2.0 children per woman, 25 to 30 percent less than the two North African states.

As can be seen from Figure 2.2, variations in fertility rates are large. Tunisia, which has had one of the more-successful economies in the region, has the lowest fertility rate, below replacement. The fertility rate in Tunisia has fallen sharply as per capita incomes have grown, females' education levels have risen, and the population has become more urbanized. Yemen has the highest fertility rate among Arab countries, almost four times that of Tunisia. It is also the poorest country in the region, with a per capita income in 2005 of $2,276 at PPP exchange rates, one-third of the per capita GDP in Tunisia. Yemen also has the lowest rates of female education, a large rural population, and, by far, the highest rates of infant mortality in the region.

Despite these differences, fertility rates have fallen across the board and are projected to continue falling out to 2020 (as shown in Figure 2.2). Rates of growth in population have also followed this downward trend. After running more than 3 percent per year in the early 1980s,

**Figure 2.2
Fertility Rates in the Arab World**

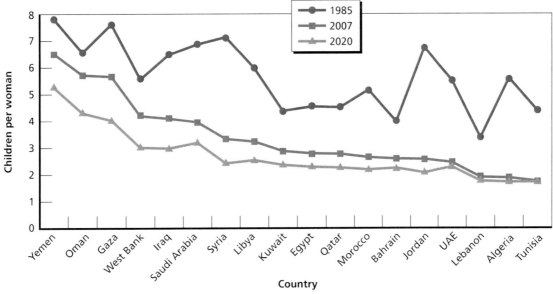

by 2007, regional population growth had fallen to a more-modest 1.7 percent per year. Population growth rates are projected to decline to 1.4 percent per year by 2020, less than half the rate of the early 1980s (as shown in Figure 2.3). However, the declines have not been uniform across countries. Despite a modest decline in its rate of population growth, at 3.8 percent, Gaza has one of the highest rates of population growth in the world. At the other end of the spectrum, Tunisia's 1.0-percent growth is almost identical to that of the United States (0.9 percent).

A number of factors affect fertility rates, including culture and religion, urbanization, and government policies. Culture and religion might play some role in these differences in fertility rates. Cultural norms, particularly in rural areas, lead many in the region to view the use of contraceptives as a sin or affront to the husband's masculinity.[2] Despite the confessional (sectarian) differences among adherents to Islam, all the various interpretations of Islam place great value on procreation.

An important determinant of fertility rates is the level of education of women. Some Muslim clerics are not strong supporters of female education and oppose mixed male-female classrooms.[3] The momentum of cultural and religious traditions, and their use by religious leaders, has worked to discourage female participation in the labor force, encourage early marriage and large families while taking a dim view of birth control. Such attitudes serve to keep fertility rates higher than they otherwise would be. This said, there is no simple correlation between the weight of religion in a given society and official policies toward birth control.

Figure 2.3
Annual Rates of Change in Population in the Arab World

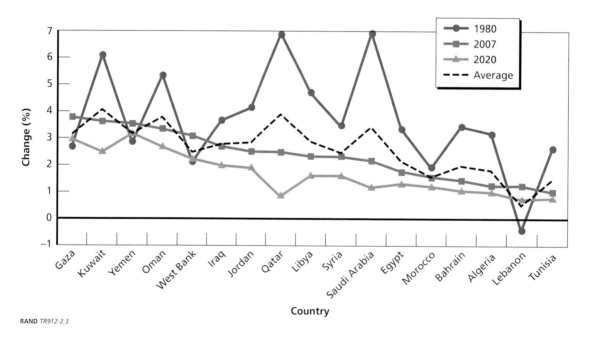

---

[2]   Najla Hassan, "Arāqīl Thaqāfiyya wa Bīiyya amam Tanīm al-Usra fī al-Yaman [Cultural and Environmental Impediments Facing Family Planning in Yemen]," *al-Hayat*, August 5, 2008.

[3]   For a particularly strong condemnation of mixed education by Syrian ulama, see the 2006 letter signed by 39 Syrian ulama calling mixed education "a pit for the corruption of values" ("Ulama Suria Yahatajūn ila al-Asad ala Qarar bi Waqf al-Qabūl bi al-Maāhid al-Sharia [Syrian Ulama Protest to al-Asad over Decision to Stop the Admissions of the Islamic Law Academies]," *Al-Arabiya.net*, July 3, 2006).

For example, the government of the Islamic Republic of Iran has strongly supported family planning.[4]

These religious and cultural factors explain some of the differences in fertility rates, but their importance should not be exaggerated. For example, the Maghreb (in particular, Morocco, Algeria, Tunisia, Libya, and Mauritania)—with its closer ties to Europe through history, cultural legacies of colonialism, tourism, trade, and immigration—has lower fertility rates than the countries of the Persian Gulf. However, in general, regional differences in fertility rates are strongly correlated with socioeconomic factors, such as income, education, and urbanization. The wealthy, highly urbanized Gulf littoral countries, such as Kuwait and Qatar, have significantly lower fertility rates than other poorer countries on the Arabian Peninsula with large rural populations, such as Yemen. Despite cultural and religious pressures for larger families, fertility rates in Arab countries have been falling—in some cases, sharply (as shown in Figure 2.2). The same factors that have resulted in declines in fertility and population growth elsewhere are also operating in the Arab world. Higher incomes provide the wherewithal for couples to better control the number of children they have and also reflect social changes that encourage smaller families.[5] Declines in child mortality rates have also contributed to lower fertility rates, as parents find it less important to have many children to ensure that some survive to provide for them in their old age. Rising levels of female education and better access to birth control have also led to lower fertility rates. Although female labor force participation rates are much lower in the Arab world than in countries elsewhere in the world with comparable per capita GDPs, increasing female participation in labor forces in Arab countries has also been accompanied by declining fertility.[6]

Urbanization is another contributing factor because it has reduced the economic benefits and increased the costs of raising children. As opposed to rural areas, where children can quickly contribute to the family's income by tending livestock or taking on other chores, in urban areas, larger families are costly, because they push up expenditures on housing, food, clothing, and education. The higher cost of living in urban settings, and the modern amenities expected by urban dwellers, make financing a marriage that much more difficult. In large cities, such as Cairo and Damascus, frustration runs high among young men who have verbally committed to marriage (*katab al-kitab*) but who cannot afford the costs of marriage, which include securing an apartment, buying furniture and appliances, and presenting the bride with jewelry (*al-shabka*).[7]

Government policies have also contributed to the variation in fertility rates. A number of the energy exporters have had the means to provide generous child-support schemes, guaranteed employment, and subsidized rents and utilities, thus offsetting the costs of bearing more children. The incentive structure created by these policies explain, in part, the higher fertility rates in such countries as the UAE and Saudi Arabia, which would be expected to have lower fertility rates given their higher educational levels and wealth and high levels of urbanization.

---

[4] Farzaneh Roudi-Fahimi, "Iran's Family Planning Program: Responding to a Nation's Needs," Washington, D.C.: Population Reference Bureau, June 2002.

[5] Higher per capita GDP is correlated with lower fertility rates. In 2007, the correlation was –0.29.

[6] For a fuller exposition of the determinants of fertility rates in the Middle East, see World Bank, *Unlocking the Employment Potential in the Middle East and North Africa: Toward a New Social Contract*, Washington, D.C., 2004, p. 51.

[7] Programming from Murasilu al-Jazira [Al Jazeera's correspondents], "al-Shabāb al-Suri wa āhirat al-Azūf an al-Zawāj [Syrian Youth and the Aversion to Marriage Phenomenon]," *Al-Jazeera.net*, October 28, 2006.

Other states have created marriage incentives, not so much to promote fertility as to head off the social pressure associated with a growing swath of young people unable to marry because of low wages and the high costs of marriage. For example, in 2004, the Syrian government pledged to provide up to $6,000 in credits to finance marriages for qualified individuals.[8]

Governments with fewer resources have generally been less pronatalist than the Persian Gulf states because of the budgetary pressures of supporting an expanding population and budgetary constraints on providing support to households with large numbers of children. Many of these states have focused on reducing birth rates. Tunisia was an early leader in supporting family planning.[9] Egypt, which faces serious stress as one of region's poorest and most-populous states, has been similarly engaged. To encourage family planning, Egypt uses televised public service announcements, subsidizes contraception, and trains and deploys thousands of female health workers to raise awareness in rural areas about the benefits of family planning.[10] The effort has met with considerable success, with Egypt's fertility rates having fallen sharply, from 4.5 births per woman in 1985 to 2.8 in 2007.[11]

Outside of family planning, policy choices in other realms also have an important, if indirect, impact on fertility rates. Along these lines, Morocco's 2004 revision of its personal-status law, *al-mudawana*, empowered women by expanding their recourse to divorce, raised the legal age of marriage, and placed restrictions on polygamy.[12] These policy choices, while not directly engaging the issue of family planning, have a long-term effect on lowering population growth.

Trends in Migration Rates in the Arab World

While not as important as fertility rates, emigration has also shaped demographic trends in the region. In oil-boom years, such as the late 1970s and early 1980s and the 2003–2008 period, workers flocked to the oil-rich Gulf states. In 1980, at the peak of the boom, the populations of these states—both immigrants and locals—grew almost 7 percent in that year. The most-recent surge in oil prices attracted a new influx of people as the Gulf states have sought workers for construction, to staff stores and restaurants, and to operate ports. In 2008, the UAE registered population growth of 6 percent, most of which came from expatriate labor.[13] However, when oil revenues drop and the demand for foreign labor declines, migrants return home.

Emigration has also reduced population growth in a number of conflict-prone Arab countries. Inhabitants have left because of unrest or in search of jobs. The most-dramatic emigrations have been driven by civil war. In the five years following the outbreak of Lebanon's civil war in 1975, the population declined as Lebanese fled the country for safer, more-prosperous regions. In 1990, following 15 years of civil war, Lebanon's population barely reached its 1975

---

[8] "6 Alāf Dullar li Kul Aris fī Suria [$6,000 for Every Groom in Syria]," *Al-Arabiya.net*, June 28, 2004.

[9] Alan Richards and John Waterbury, *A Political Economy of the Middle East*, 2nd ed., Boulder, Colo.: Westview Press, 1996, pp. 86–87.

[10] Amina Khairi, "al-Tiliviziyūn Laab Dawrān Kabīran . . . al-Tamwīl al-Ajanabī Yansaib min Tanīm al-Nasl fī Misr [The Television Played a Major Role: Foreign Funding Is Falling Back in Family Planning in Egypt]," *al-Hayat*, October 17, 2006.

[11] Scott Moreland, *Egypt's Population Program: Assessing 25 Years of Family Planning*, Washington, D.C.: U.S. Agency for International Development, March 2006.

[12] Farzaneh Roudi-Fahimi and Mary Mederios Kent, "Challenges and Opportunities: The Population of the Middle East and North Africa," *Population Bulletin*, Vol. 62, No. 2, June 2007, p. 9.

[13] "UAE Population to Grow 6% in 2009," *Emirates Business*, May 19, 2009.

total.[14] Changes in the population of the West Bank and Gaza have also been driven by conflict. Following the 1967 war, when Israel occupied these two territories, the population fell 20 percent as Palestinians fled out of fear, left because they did not want to live under an Israeli occupation, or emigrated looking for work. Population growth slowed markedly again in the late 1970s as Palestinians went to the Persian Gulf to work. Following the 1990–1991 Gulf War, the population of the West Bank and Gaza rose when Palestinians were expelled from Kuwait and other Gulf states. Population growth in Iraq has also been affected by emigration. Under Saddam Hussein, hundreds of thousands of Iraqis left the country for economic and political reasons. Although the precise numbers are disputed, since the U.S. invasion, another wave of Iraqis, also numbering in the hundreds of thousands, has left the country, fleeing from the violence.[15]

Beyond affecting gross population numbers, migration also affects fertility. Most migrants are males, often relatively young. Many workers in the Persian Gulf states stay for 24 months or longer because of contractual stipulations and the cost of traveling home. Working abroad might delay marriage or, in the case of married workers, reduce pregnancies, as young couples remain apart for extended periods of time. Then again, opportunities for young men from poorer Arab countries, such as Egypt, to work in the Gulf and quickly build savings can help to facilitate marriage among those who would otherwise have to work many years in their home country to save the money needed to marry.

Population, Fertility, and Migration Trends in Israel and the West Bank and Gaza

Although Israel is not a part of the Arab world, the Palestinian territories are. Population, fertility, and migration trends for Israelis and Palestinians are important components of the conflict and discussions on coming to a resolution. Israelis and Palestinians perceive demographic trends in highly political terms: Both argue that the ethnic group that is in the majority will have a stronger claim on territory. Populating the land is equated with rights of ownership and control. Perhaps not surprisingly, demographic trends in both groups—Israelis and Palestinians—are somewhat anomalous compared to other countries or areas in the region. Israel has a higher fertility rate than Tunisia, even though Israel's per capita GDP is almost four times higher. In contrast to all other countries in the region, population growth rates in the West Bank and Gaza have risen since 1980. Gaza now has the highest rate of population growth in the region, with the West Bank not far behind (as shown in Figure 2.3).

Changes in the population of the West Bank and Gaza have been driven by fertility rates but heavily influenced by migration. Because of historically higher levels of education and a better public health care system than in many other areas in the region, Palestinian mortality rates are relatively low and life expectancy correspondingly high, running 73 years.[16] After falling in the 1980s, fertility rates rose again in the 1990s, an uncommon development. No other country in the region has experienced an increase in fertility rates in the past four decades.

The conflict with Israel appears to have had some effect on fertility, primarily through the effects of closure and conflict. In light of the high levels of insecurity in the West Bank and

[14] According to the United Nations Population Database, Lebanon's population stood at 2,735,000 in 1975 and 2,974,000 in 1990 (United Nations Department of Economic and Social Affairs, *World Urbanization Prospects: The 2005 Revision*, New York, POP/DB/WUP/Rev. 2005, October 2006).

[15] United Nations High Commissioner for Refugees, "Statistics on Displaced Iraqis Around the World," April 1, 2007.

[16] Central Intelligence Agency, *The World Factbook*, Washington, D.C., updated weekly.

Gaza and high rates of unemployment, women are more apt to stay home and less apt to partic-ipate in the labor force than they once did. Attending school has become more difficult. Some indicators suggest that adolescents are less likely to go to school. All these factors are correlated with higher fertility rates and appear to have contributed to an increase in Palestinian fertili-ty.[17] The political element, the desire on the part of some Palestinians to become a majority of the population in the area of Israel, the West Bank, and Gaza as a unit is difficult to quantify but might have had some effect on the desire to have more children. Palestinians living outside the West Bank and Gaza have lower fertility rates than those within, even lower than the aver-age in the Arab world.[18] They also have higher incomes and more access to education.

Economic and social factors fail to fully explain Israeli fertility rates. Although Israel is primarily an immigrant state, most immigrants are quickly acculturated, as in the United States. During the 1950s, Jewish immigrants from North Africa had fertility rates two or three times higher than those of immigrants from Europe. By 1990, the daughters of immi-grants from North Africa and Europe had fairly similar fertility rates. In contrast, very sharp differences in fertility exist between very religious and less religious or secular Jewish Israe-lis. Between the periods 1980–1982 and 1995–1996, the total fertility rate rose from 6.49 to 7.61 children per woman for the ultraorthodox while it fell from 2.61 to 2.27 for the rest of Israeli Jews.[19]

Some have argued that higher fertility rates among the ultraorthodox will have a signifi-cant impact on the Israeli politics of the future. This assertion is questionable: In a society as dynamic as Israel's, the ideological positions of parents affect but do not determine those of their children. Moreover, migration is likely to continue to play a major role in determining the size and composition of Israel's Jewish population. The immigration of citizens of the former Soviet Union since 1989 increased the population of Israel by upwards of a fifth. This popula-tion tends to be more secular in orientation, yet more supportive of political parties that have taken a tougher line toward Palestinian demands.

According to the U.S. Census Bureau, the total projected Arab population in Israel, the West Bank, and Gaza will exceed the projected Jewish population within a few years. As of 2005, the Arab population was already 48 percent of the total population living in these areas, up from 43 percent in 1995 (Figure 2.4). Although Israel's official projections of its population in 2020 estimate only a modest decrease in the share of the Jewish population inside Israel,[20] this assumes continued immigration of Jews from abroad.[21] While the size of the respective populations does not equal political control, the increase in the share of the non-Jewish popu-

---

[17] Kevin F. McCarthy, *The Palestine Refugee Issue: One Perspective*, Santa Monica, Calif.: RAND Corporation, DRU-1358-GMSEC, 1996.

[18] Kevin F. McCarthy and Brian Nichiporuk, "Demography," in RAND Palestinian State Study Team, *Building a Success-ful Palestinian State*, Santa Monica, Calif.: RAND Corporation, MG-146-1-DCR, 2004, pp. 73–106.

[19] Eli Berman, "Sect, Subsidy, and Sacrifice: An Economist's View of Ultra-Orthodox Jews," *Quarterly Journal of Econom-ics*, Vol. 115, No. 3, August 2000, pp. 905–953, as cited in Philippe Fargues, "Protracted National Conflict and Fertility Change: Palestinians and Israelis in the Twentieth Century," *Population and Development Review*, Vol. 26, No. 3, Septem-ber 2000, p. 451.

[20] Israeli Central Bureau of Statistics, *Projections of Israel's Population Until 2020*, c. 1997, Table 2.

[21] Israeli Central Bureau of Statistics, 1997, Chapter 5, offers greater detail on the bureau's assumptions in preparing its estimates.

Figure 2.4
Ethnic Composition of the Population of Israel, the West Bank, and Gaza

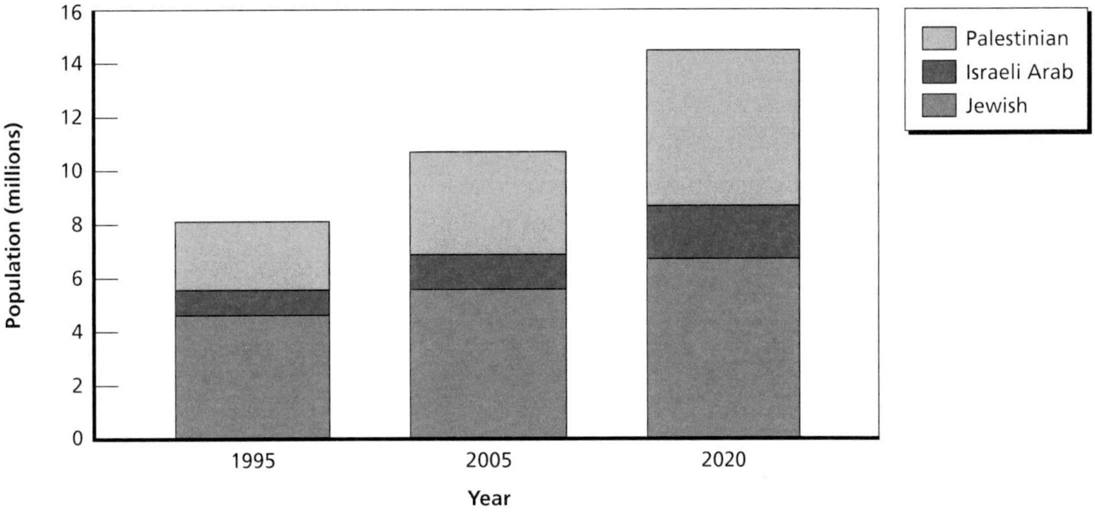

SOURCE: U.S. Census Bureau, 2008.
RAND *TR912-2.4*

lation of the region makes Israeli control of the West Bank and Gaza even more questionable as the demographic balance shifts.

What Are the Implications of These Demographic Trends?

These demographic trends have implications for the Arab world, particularly because of resource constraints related to water and food.

Water. At first glance, the Arab world does not appear to be a densely populated region. Population densities are far below those in East Asia and Europe. However, climate and topography work to keep this population concentrated in a few pockets of territory. Outside of Antarctica, the Arab world is the most arid region on earth. The Sahara and the Arabian deserts are the two largest deserts in the world. The Sahara is seven times larger than the Gobi, the third-largest desert, while the Arabian desert is twice as large.[22] Historically, only Bedouin tribes lived in the desert; most of the population of the region lived along the rivers, especially the Nile, the Tigris, and Euphrates; the seacoasts; or more-temperate highland areas, such as those in Lebanon, Morocco, Syria, Yemen, and the Kurdish areas of Iraq. Although the populations of the desert kingdoms of Saudi Arabia and the Persian Gulf states have soared over the past century, to this day, the populations of this region remain concentrated in the nondesert areas. In these areas, population densities are often very high. Although the population density for Egypt as a whole is 76.3 people per square kilometer, 99 percent of the population is squeezed into the 4 percent of Egypt's land area that borders the Nile or the Mediterranean

---

[22] "Principal Deserts of the World," *infoplease*, 2007.

Sea.[23] Population densities along the Nile run as high as 1,200 people per square kilometer, one of the highest densities in the world.[24]

In light of the arid nature of the region, it is not surprising that agriculture depends on irrigation. Agriculture is the major consumer of water in the region, accounting for 93 percent of total water use, in contrast to a more-typical pattern of 85 percent of water use in developing countries in general.[25]

The combination of rapid population growth, irrigation, and the arid nature of the region have resulted in severe pressures on water supplies. The biggest problem is overuse of aquifers. Outside of Egypt, the region is already consuming 16 percent more water per year than is being replenished.[26] According to the World Bank, Saudi Arabia and Kuwait have been withdrawing ten times more water from aquifers than is being replenished through rainfall; Gaza is taking three times more. The only country in the region that is close to exploiting its aquifers in a sustainable manner is Morocco.[27] At current rates of extraction, a number of aquifers will run dry over the next few decades, including some in Jordan, Kuwait, and Saudi Arabia. If patterns of water consumption should continue on the current trajectory, by 2025, the Arab world, excluding Egypt, will be consuming 39 percent more water than is available on a sustained basis. Egypt, which currently has a buffer of 11 percent, would also be consuming 8 percent more water in 2025 than is available on a sustainable basis.[28]

Despite this dire projection based on the assumption of business as usual, water is unlikely to become a binding constraint on growth if policies are adjusted. The studies by the World Bank, the International Food Policy Research Institute, and the International Water Management Institute contain alternative scenarios that assume better water-management practices, which result in sustainable water utilization on a region-wide basis. Key policy measures include setting prices so as to cover full costs of the water and to reflect its scarcity value, more investment in sewage-treatment systems, and more-efficient irrigation practices. Somewhat surprisingly, under these assumptions, it is not necessary to reduce the area being irrigated to provide more water to household and industrial users. Rather, improvements in irrigation efficiency are projected to release enough water from agricultural users to satisfy increased demand from other users.

Even if one does not use these optimistic assumptions, water-imposed constraints on economic growth will be localized. In countries that rely heavily on irrigation, modest diversions of water from irrigation to other users would satisfy increased household and industrial demand at the expense of a modest drop in grain output. Even regions that rely on aquifers, such as the West Bank and Saudi Arabia, can satisfy increased demand for nonagricultural water use by reducing the water available for irrigation. As agriculture accounts for only

---

[23] Economic Commission for Africa, "Egypt," *National Information and Communication Infrastructure (NICI) Policies and Plans (e-strategies)*, undated web page.

[24] Central Intelligence Agency, "Egypt," *World Factbook*, last updated January 13, 2011.

[25] Mark W. Rosegrant, Ximing Cai, and Sarah A. Cline, "The Future of Water and Food in the Middle East and North Africa: Outlook to 2025," Washington, D.C.: International Food Policy Research Institute and Institute and International Water Management Institute, 2002, slide 15.

[26] Rosegrant, Cai, and Cline, 2002, slide 17.

[27] Jamal Saghir, "Strategic Provision of Water Sector Services in MENA," presentation, Mediterranean Development Forum, Washington, D.C., March 6–8, 2000, slide 7.

[28] Rosegrant, Cai, and Cline, 2002, slide 17.

5.2 percent of Saudi GDP, the diversion of water from agriculture to other uses would not have a major economic impact.

The West Bank is different. Although agriculture used to account for only 7 percent of economic output in the West Bank and Gaza, it has been an important residual employer and source of income and food, especially during times when Israel imposes more-stringent controls on movement by Palestinians. Agriculture accounts for 64 percent of water consumption in the West Bank and Gaza. A substantial decline in water for agriculture would hurt the economies of these territories.[29]

Regions facing more-serious problems include Gaza, Jordan, and the Gulf states. The latter are already using desalinization plants, a very expensive source of water, to satisfy urban demand. Gaza and Jordan do not have the energy wealth that makes desalinization affordable to the Gulf states. However, Gaza will almost certainly need to turn to desalinization, and the West Bank might need to use this source of water as well.[30]

Throughout the region, the cost of investing in and operating improved irrigation and water-treatment facilities, both for potable water and for sewerage, are sizable. Currently, these investments are running on the order of 1 to 2 percent of GDP and 40 to 45 percent of total public investment on an annual basis, this for systems in which water quality and water availability on a per capita basis are declining. Although the costs are not enough to derail growth, investments and operating costs for water systems will continue to form a major component of public expenditure, unless much more-aggressive policy changes are made to operate these systems on a total cost-recovery basis.

Food. Food is a highly sensitive political issue in the region. Providing adequate food has been a concern of local rulers since biblical times. Affordability has been an issue for almost as long. Price controls and food subsidies also date back to biblical times. More recently, bread shortages and the removal of subsidies on key foodstuffs have generated strong challenges to governments of Arab states.

Rapid population growth and food-subsidy programs that discourage domestic production, coupled with limited water resources, have turned the region into a major importer of food, especially grains. Table 2.1 shows imports of agricultural products for a number of the countries in the region and the share of food in total imports. As can be seen, imports of food account for 12 to 18 percent of total imports in populous states, such as Algeria, Egypt, and Saudi Arabia, and from 8 to 13 percent of imports in most of the remaining countries.

Given the severe pressures on water resources and continued population growth, the region will be increasing rather than reducing the volume of imports of food in the coming decades. Whether food imports will become an increasing burden on the local economies—crowding out imports of machinery and equipment and other goods needed to foster economic growth—or growth in exports of goods and services make possible sizable imports of food without constraining imports of other items will be a key factor in the future economic health of these countries. These countries' ability to foster sustained growth in exports will be the key to generating the foreign currency that will make food supplies and the affordability of food imports a problem of the past.

---

[29] Mark Bernstein, David G. Groves, and Amber Moreen, "Water," in RAND Palestinian State Study Team, *Building a Successful Palestinian State*, Santa Monica, Calif.: RAND Corporation, MG-146-1-DCR, 2007, pp. 163–221.

[30] Bernstein, Groves, and Moreen, 2007.

Table 2.1
Agricultural Imports in the Arab World, 2007

Country	Value (millions $)	Share of Total Country Imports (%)
Algeria	4,944	17.9
Bahrain	574	5.0
Egypt	4,451	16.5
Jordan	1,889	14.0
Kuwait	2,659	12.4
Lebanon	1,741	18.6
Morocco	3,263	10.3
Oman	1,434	8.9
Qatar	1,082	4.6
Saudi Arabia	11,222	12.4
Syrian Arab Republic	1,594	10.9
Tunisia	1,617	8.5
UAE	7,044	5.5
Yemen	1,982	23.3
Total	45,496	10.3

SOURCE: United Nations Commodity Trade Statistics Database, *UN Comtrade*, queried September 17, 2009.

How Valid Are the Demographic Trends' Forecasts?

Demographic projections for the region all assume continued declines in fertility and population growth rates. Demographers, both at the United Nations and at the U.S. Census Bureau, predict that the same factors that have served to slow population growth rates in other parts of the world will continue to push rates down in the Arab world as well. How reliable are these forecasts?

The experience of the past three decades provides strong support for the assumption that fertility rates will continue to decline. Although rates have been higher in Arab countries than in other regions with similar levels of per capita income, the trends—even in poorer countries—are mimicking patterns elsewhere in the world. Fertility rates have (belatedly) begun to fall very sharply, including in the Persian Gulf states (as shown in Figure 2.2).

The potential wild card in forecasts of slowing population growth would be lower-than-expected growth in per capita GDP, the subject of the next two chapters. Fertility rates have risen in Iraq, the West Bank, and Gaza during periods of severe economic stress, when opportunities for further education, especially for young women, are reduced. Although demographic trends in Gaza and the West Bank are also skewed by the conflict with Israel, fertility tends to fall more rapidly in countries experiencing economic expansion than in countries whose economies are performing poorly. Although causality probably runs both ways—that is, the pressures resulting from rapid population growth might slow growth in per capita GDP—if the coming years are marked by slow economic growth, population growth in the region might fail to fall, keeping the pot of demographic pressures bubbling well into the future.

Demographic Trends Within Populations in the Arab World

Beyond population, fertility, and migration trends, we are also interested in trends within the populations in the Arab world—especially trends in the age structure of the population, trends in urbanization, and trends in ethnic and religious mix.

The Influx of Youth into Labor Markets

Declining fertility rates not only lead to a slowdown in population growth; they also lead to a shift in the age structure of the population when they occur in tandem with stable or rising life expectancy. During the past several decades, the Arab world has experienced a "youth bulge." High fertility rates coupled with dramatic reductions in infant and child mortality resulted in an explosion in the number of children in the region. These children have been coming of age, leading to a large influx of young people into local labor markets.

While the rate of population growth in the Arab world is projected to slow to 1.4 percent in 2020 from 1.7 percent in 2006, the pool of potential laborers is projected to continue to grow rapidly. Between 2006 and 2020, the working-age population is projected to rise by one-third. As this bulge of young people comes of working age, the pressures governments in the region face are shifting away from providing education and health services for a very youthful population to creating employment opportunities for young adults. This bulge provides both opportunities to local governments—with the influx of more, better-educated labor into the economies occurring as the number of dependents per worker is falling—and challenges; if many young adults, especially young men, continue to find that their expectations are not met, outbreaks of violence, civil strife, and crime will continue.

Figure 2.5 represents the projected increase in young men entering the labor force between 1996 and 2020. As shown, the size of the 2020 cohort exceeds the 1996 cohort by close to 40 percent. Although the influx in North Africa stabilizes by 2007, reflecting the lower birth rates in that region, in the Near East, these cohorts continue to rise. Consequently, the pressure on local labor markets from this influx of young men is only just beginning to ease in North Africa and will not cease in the Near East until 2020. Through 2020, the number of men reaching retirement age is low: only 3.8 million in 2007. Consequently, the number of net additions to the labor force does not begin to slow until 2020, when the number of retirees hits 6.3 million.

The acculturation of these large cohorts of young men is one of the most-difficult problems facing these societies. Young men between the ages of 15 and 30 are more prone to violence than any other social group. In the countries of North Africa, the Levant, and the Persian Gulf, social and economic forces combine to exacerbate the problem of acculturation. Over the past two decades, growth in jobs has lagged increases in the labor force as the heavy hand of the state has discouraged the creation of private-sector jobs, while fiscal pressures have slowed growth in public-sector jobs. For social and economic reasons, educated youth have preferred public-sector jobs. Arab societies have given public-sector employment higher status because such employment is more secure than those in the private sector, because desk jobs in government are less onerous than most private-sector jobs, and because employees are guaranteed a

Figure 2.5
Population of Young Men Entering the Labor Force

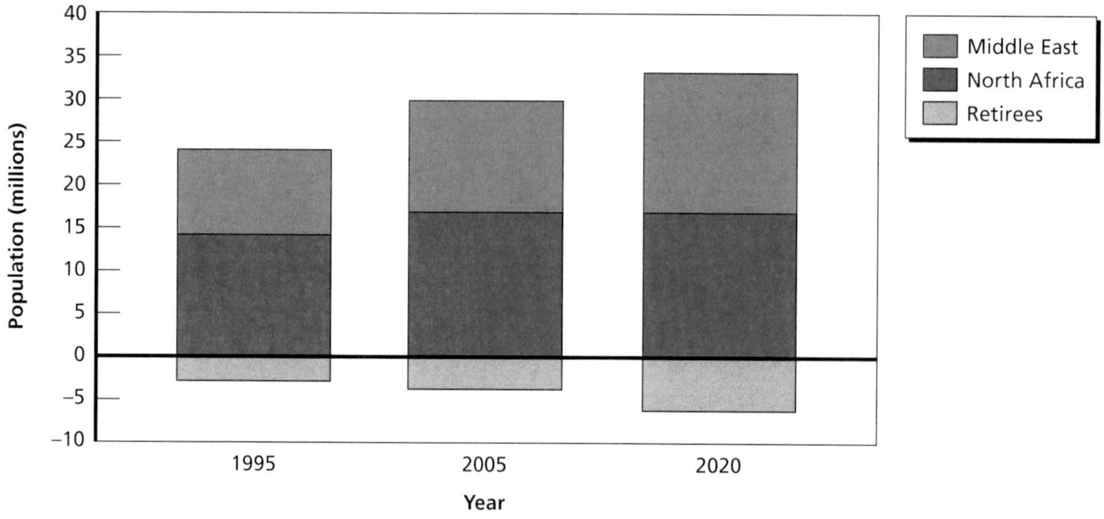

SOURCE: U.S. Census Bureau, 2008.
RAND *TR912-2.5*

salary (in contrast to the more-precarious incomes available from the private sector, especially self-employment). Consequently, young men often choose to remain idle while waiting for an opening in the government bureaucracy rather than seek work as day laborers or engage in small-scale businesses. A tradition of family support also permits youth to remain unemployed for much longer periods than in other, poorer societies.

Not all people of working age seek employment. Some are engaged in education; others do housework; some are ill; and, as noted above, some are idle, although few societies condone idleness among working-age adults. Labor force participation ratios—the proportion of people of working age who work or would like to work—measure the share of the working-age population in the labor force, either working or looking for work. While male labor force participation rates in the Arab countries are similar to those in other regions in the world, women work outside the home much less frequently than elsewhere. Taking a simple average of the latest figures available, only 25.4 percent of the female population between 15 and 64 participate in the labor force in this region (Figure 2.6). As a point of comparison, female participation rates in Colombia ran 47.1 percent in 2006; in the United States, it was 67 percent. Because women have low rates of participation in work outside the home, labor force participation ratios in the Arab countries are the lowest in the world.[31] In Saudi Arabia, women's educational gains tend to run into the dead hand of tradition. Seventy-six percent of unemployed females in the kingdom are university graduates, the opposite profile of their unemployed male counterparts.[32]

---

[31] International Labour Organization, *Key Indicators of the Labour Market, 2001–2002*, New York: Routledge, 2002.

[32] "al-Saudia: 76 percent min al-Āilāt Jāmiīāt wa Ghālabīyat al-Ālīn min al-amlat al-Thanawiyya [Saudi Arabia: 76 Percent of Unemployed Women Are University Graduates and the Majority of Unemployed Males Are from the Ranks of High School Graduates]," *Asharq al-Awsat*, September 15, 2008.

Figure 2.6
Labor Force Participation Rates, Total and by Gender

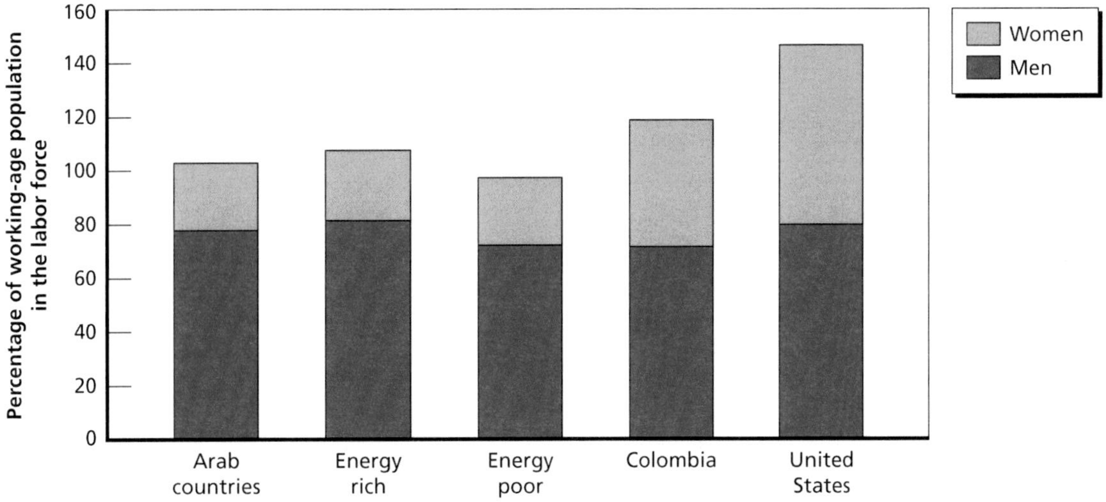

SOURCE: Calculated from individual country data from the International Labour Organization, accessed March 11, 2008.

RAND *TR912-2.6*

Unwillingness to allow these women greater access to the labor market makes them a "major and underutilized human resource."[33]

Because of a slow but steady increase in female labor force participation ratios, labor force participation rates in the Arab world are likely to rise over the course of the next two decades. Thus, the labor force will grow even more rapidly than the increase in numbers of people of working age. Three factors will drive more participation by women in the labor force. First, as educational levels rise, more women will work outside the home. Women with higher levels of education are both more marketable and more interested in working outside the home. Rising levels of female education have already been accompanied by increases in female labor force participation rates. Second, women in urban areas participate in the labor market more than women in rural areas. In urban areas, women generally must work outside the home if they are to provide additional income to the family. As Arab countries continue to become more urban, this trend will likely result in greater female participation rates in the workforce. Finally, higher levels of education and greater urbanization result in smaller families. As family sizes shrink, women are more likely to work outside the home.

Continued Growth in Urbanization

Because of constraints on land and water, rural areas have long ceased to provide attractive employment prospects in the region. Men, especially young men, have been steadily migrating to urban centers for the past several decades, bringing or establishing families after getting a start. Although steady employment is not readily available, the occasional employment available in urban areas generally pays better and is more frequent than seasonal work in farming communities.

---

[33] Mona Al-Munajjed, *Women in Saudi Arabia Today*, New York: St. Martin's Press, 1997; Roula Baki, "Gender-Segregated Education in Saudi Arabia: Its Impact on Social Norms [and] the Saudi Labor Market," *Education Policy Analysis Archives*, Vol. 12, No. 28, June 17, 2004.

Figure 2.7 shows past and future urban and rural populations of the Near East and North Africa, computed from percentages of the population that live in urban areas from the United Nations and figures on total population from the U.S. Census Bureau.[34] As can be seen, the United Nations projects little growth in rural populations in either North Africa or the Near East through 2020, but urban populations are projected to increase by two-fifths. As a consequence, the share of the population in urban areas jumps, rising to 60 percent of the total population in North Africa and 67 percent of the population of the Near East.

Historically, most migrants flocked to the capital cities. However, now that Cairo, Baghdad, Damascus, and Algiers are suffering from overcrowding, immigrants are shifting toward smaller urban areas closer to their birthplaces. In Morocco, Marrakech and Fez are growing rapidly. In Egypt, such cities as Al Mahallah, Aswan, Al Minya, and Ismailia are absorbing migrants that would likely have settled in Cairo a decade earlier. In Iraq, Mosul and Kirkuk play a similar role. In many cases, these second-tier cities are now growing more rapidly than the capital cities.[35] Although this dynamic has served to reduce some of the pressures on the capitals, it shifts the burden to second-tier cities that do not have the infrastructure, housing, or capacity for the delivery of public services of a typical capital city. And while it is true that the infrastructure of most capital cities is under pressure because of rising populations, it is also generally cheaper to add capacity to these existing systems than to build new systems from scratch. The cost of improving or providing these systems in second-tier cities places additional pressures on budgets.

Failure to improve conditions in second-tier cities is likely to have high costs insofar as urban squalor has proved a breeding ground for resentment and violence. Many men from the region who have become terrorists have some university training and have lived in second-

Figure 2.7
Urban and Rural Populations of the Near East and North Africa

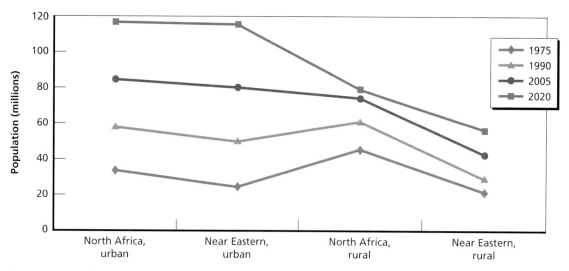

SOURCES: United Nations Department of Economic and Social Affairs, 2006; U.S. Census Bureau, 2008.
RAND *TR912-2.7*

---

[34] United Nations Department of Economic and Social Affairs, 2006.

[35] United Nations Department of Economic and Social Affairs, Population Division, *World Urbanization Prospects: The 1999 Revision*, New York, ST/ESA/SER. A/194, 2001, pp. 79–82.

tier cities. The Egyptian members of al Qaeda have generally not been from Cairo.[36] Tangier and Tetouan, not the capital, Rabat, have been important recruiting cities for the Moroccan Islamic Combatant Group (Groupe Islamique Combattant Marocain, or GICM) that was responsible for the Casablanca and Madrid bombings.[37] The former head of the Armed Islamic Group (Groupe Islamique Armé, or GIA), the Algerian insurgent group, is from Boufarik, not from Algiers. He continued to operate from that town until he was killed in 2002.[38]

Rapid urbanization poses a number of other challenges to the regimes in the region. Having large numbers of frequently idle young men who congregate in densely populated housing blocks or in makeshift housing at the edge of urban areas is a security risk. The provision of water, sanitation, transportation, and the quality of the housing stock in these immigrant areas are generally poor. On a daily basis, these immigrants are confronted with the failure of the government to provide minimal services. Their most-frequent interaction with the government is often through exposure to the police, who treat them with suspicion and often hostility. These young men find that alternative institutions, especially local mosques and religious organizations, do a better job of addressing their needs than does the government. These institutions provide food, shelter, and, in some instances, jobs for recently arrived migrants. They also provide a social network for youth who are accustomed to supportive family and clans in their native villages.

Regardless of the preferred policy outcome, experience shows that urbanization can be slowed but cannot be stopped. With the exception of Egypt and Iraq, the countryside provides little in the way of employment outside of subsistence agriculture. (In those two countries, a number of rural inhabitants are engaged in providing local services, such as transport, construction, and trade. Some light manufacturing and handicrafts are also located in rural areas.) The jobs of the future are in the cities. As a result, governments in the region will face a continued influx of migrants seeking a better life there.

Changes in Religious and Ethnic Mix
Over the next two decades, the composition of Arab world's population will change not only in terms of age and in terms of where that population chooses to live but also in terms of its religious and ethnic mix. The rising or declining fortunes of the various ethnic and religious minorities in the region have contributed to civil strife in a number of countries, including Algeria, Egypt, Iraq, Lebanon, and Morocco. In some countries, these ongoing shifts are likely to exacerbate tensions and will play a major role in determining future political trends in the region.

The Decline of Religious Minorities. Historically, the Middle East has been a region of many religions and ethnicities. The Arabian peninsula is home to the holiest shrines of Islam: Mecca and Medina. Jerusalem is the center of the Jewish faith, and Israel and Palestine hold the earliest sites of Christianity. The Bahai faith was founded in Iran, but its holiest center is now in Israel. The three monotheistic faiths are further divided into many sects and denomina-

[36] Daniel Benjamin and Steven Simon, *The Age of Sacred Terror*, New York: Random House, 2002.

[37] Benjamin Keating, "In the Spotlight: Moroccan Combatant Group (GICM)," Center for Defense Information, May 21, 2004.

[38] "Top Islamist Militant 'Killed' in Algeria," *BBC News*, February 9, 2002; "Top Algerian Terrorist Killed," *People's Daily On-Line*, February 10, 2002.

tions. These groups live close together throughout the region. Theological and political differences within the faiths have been the source of much violence.

The region is becoming more Muslim and, therefore, more religiously homogeneous. Under Ottoman rule, monotheistic faiths, such as Christianity and Judaism, were tolerated, although they held the status of *dhimmis*, a kind of second-class citizenship.[39] Periodically, the Middle East was a refuge for Jews insofar as Jewish communities suffered less persecution there than in Christian Europe. Some of these communities were large: In the 19th century, roughly one-fourth of the population of Baghdad was Jewish.[40] However, by the 1950s, the ascendancy of Arab nationalism, the perception that Jews were agents of colonial powers, and the creation of the state of Israel contributed to anti-Jewish pogroms. By the end of 1960s, for all intents and purposes, all of the ancient Jewish communities in Arab countries had emigrated to Israel. For example, the Jewish community in Egypt, which had been concentrated in Alexandria and Cairo, fell from 8,561 in 1960 to 794 in 1986, according to U.S. Census Bureau figures.[41]

The Arab Christian population has also declined, although in relative rather than absolute terms. Today, the total Arab Christian population is estimated at 6 million to 7 million, or about 6 percent of the population of the countries in which Christians are most prominent: Egypt, Lebanon, Syria, Iraq, Jordan, and Palestine.[42] These communities are ancient. The very first Christian communities were found in Palestine and in what today are Lebanon and Syria.

As a share of the total Palestinian population, Christians have been in decline for more than 100 years.[43] During the first Arab-Israeli War in 1949, many Palestinian Christians left Israel. After the conquest of the West Bank in 1968 and the oil boom of the 1970s, disproportionate numbers of Palestinian Christians, who tend to be well educated, emigrated to the Persian Gulf or the West to work. In the 1980s and 1990s, this ethnic group continued to leave Palestine, fleeing from the violence and seeking better economic opportunities. This group has a lower birth rate than Muslim Palestinians: Fertility rates among Palestinian Christians average 2.6 children per woman as opposed to 6.2 per Muslim woman.[44] Because of emigration and a lower birth rate, the share of Christians among Palestinians has fallen from 11.3 percent in Palestine in 1914 to between 1.1 and 2.4 percent in the West Bank and Gaza today.[45]

The Lebanese Christian community, which is primarily Maronite or Greek Orthodox, has been hardier than its Palestinian counterpart, but trends are similar. The Lebanese Christian population has declined from an official figure of 55 percent of the total in 1921, the year in which the state of Lebanon was established, to an estimated 35 percent in 1990 and 25 per-

---

[39] Paying a poll tax was justified on the basis that it served as compensation for not contributing to the defense of the "state" insofar as minorities were not always eligible to serve in Muslim armies. See also Barbara Harff, "Minorities, Rebellion, and Repression in North Africa and the Middle East," in Ted Robert Gurr, ed., *Minorities at Risk: A Global View of Ethnopolitical Conflicts*, Washington, D.C.: U.S. Institute of Peace, 1993, p. 251.

[40] Charles Tripp, *A History of Iraq*, Cambridge, UK: Cambridge University Press, 2002.

[41] U.S. Census Bureau, 2008.

[42] Philippe Fargues, "The Arab Christians of the Middle East: A Demographic Perspective," in Andrea Pacini, ed., *Christian Communities in the Arab Middle East: The Challenge of the Future*, Oxford: Clarendon Press, 1998, pp. 48–66.

[43] Fargues, 1998.

[44] Fargues, 1998.

[45] Fargues, 1998.

cent in 2000.[46] After the start of the civil war in 1975, many Lebanese emigrated, especially the better-educated, wealthier Christian minority: Of 700,000 emigrants since 1975, 500,000 were Christian.[47] In addition, like their Palestinian Christian counterparts, Lebanese Christians have lower fertility rates than Muslim Lebanese, especially the poorer Shi'ite minority in the south and east of the country. As a consequence, the Shi'ite community in Lebanon has risen from 17 percent of the population in 1920 to become the largest ethnic community in Lebanon, accounting for more than one-third of the total population.[48] Lebanon has become considerably less Christian, and its Muslim population has become more Shi'ite and less Sunni.

Syria is also home to historically Christian communities; roughly 6.5 percent of the population consists of Greek or Armenian Orthodox.[49] Like the Christian communities elsewhere in the region, the communities have shrunk as adherents have emigrated to Western Europe and North America. Then again, Syria has also become an important host for many Iraqi Christian refugees fleeing violence or religious persecution.[50]

In 2003, Iraq's Christian communities numbered about 600,000 people, less than 3 percent of the total population. Iraq's Christians include the Chaldean-Assyrians (the largest sect), Armenians, Syrian Catholics, and Syrian Orthodox. The Christian community in Iraq has declined because of emigration. The first major exodus was in the 1990s, but Christians have been leaving Iraq since the invasion, fleeing the violence, because the community has been targeted by insurgents.[51] Fertility rates in this group are also relatively low.

The Coptic community in Egypt has been somewhat more resilient than Christians elsewhere in the region. Like other Christian communities in the region, the Copts tend to be better educated than Egyptian society as a whole. In fact, the academic achievement of Coptic students has led to an association in Egypt between the community and what Egyptians call *Kuliat al-Qima*—a reference to the most-competitive university programs, including medicine, engineering, and pharmacology. Estimates of the size of the community vary widely,[52] but Copts are believed to comprise between 5 and 10 percent of the Egypt's total population. With declining fertility rates in Egypt's Muslim population, the Coptic share of Egypt's population should no longer decline as rapidly as in the past.

In the next few decades, Islam appears destined to become even more dominant in the region. Emigration of Christians from Iraq and Lebanon might have slowed, but it has not stopped. The emigration of Palestinian Christians continues. Sizable religious minorities are an important source of pluralism. They provide a countervailing force to calls for the creation of ecclesiastical states in the region. As these populations decline or disappear, the absence of

---

[46] "Guide: Christians in the Middle East," *BBC News*, December 15, 2005.

[47] Fouad Daoud Abi-Esber, *The Rise and Fall of Christian Minorities in Lebanon*, Sydney: Academic Research, 2005.

[48] Harff, 1993, pp. 239–240.

[49] Ray J. Mouawad, "Syria and Iraq—Repression: Disappearing Christians of the Middle East," *Middle East Quarterly*, Vol. VIII, No. 1, Winter 2001, pp. 51–50; Fargues, 1998.

[50] Katherine Zoepf, "Many Christians Flee Iraq with Syria the Haven of Choice," *New York Times*, August 5, 2004.

[51] Salim Abraham, "Iraqi Christians Flee to Syria Because of Pressure from Muslim Extremists," Associated Press, August 2004.

[52] For example, compare Fargues, 1998, with the Central Intelligence Agency (CIA) *World Factbook*. According to Fargues, Copts' share of Egypt's total population fell from 7.3 percent in 1960 to 5.9 percent in 1986, and their share of the total Egyptian population continued to decline in the intervening two decades. According to the CIA *World Factbook*, Copts still comprise a much larger share of Egypt's population: 9 percent in 2006 (CIA, 2008).

non-Muslim populations bolsters the position of Islamists calling for the primacy of religion in the state,[53] weakening the position of those who argue for a more-secular state.

Despite the absolute or relative decline of non-Muslim religious communities, an increasingly Muslim region will still not be ideologically homogeneous. Although one of the trends of the past two decades has been the rise in the numbers of more-religious, conservative Muslims, a countervailing trend has been the continued "secularization" of parts of the region, especially in those Arab countries that have enjoyed higher rates of economic growth. Patterns of fertility, dress, and labor force participation among younger urban women in Tunisia, Lebanon, Algeria, and Jordan are very different from those in their mothers' generation, let alone their grandmothers'. Although these young women are generally observant, they have more freedom, higher levels of education, and different views on procreation and their role in the home than did previous generations. Arab youth, male and female, are influenced by popular Arab culture, which encompasses but is not limited to Islam. Young Arabs are also aware of Western trends in dress, movies, and television. And while these cultural trends are not necessarily un-Islamic, they do introduce ideas and beliefs that contrast considerably with those espoused by Islamists.

Uneasy Relations Between Arab and Non-Arab Ethnic Groups. The region, although populated primarily by Arabic speakers, is also home to a number of other ethnic groups. The largest ethnic groups are the Berbers in North Africa and the Kurds, who live in an area extending across Iraq, Syria, and into Iran and Turkey. The Berbers were the dominant indigenous group in North Africa (outside of Egypt) at the time of the Arab conquest in the eighth century. They intermarried with the Arabs to such an extent that there is no pure Arab population in the region. For example, 80 percent of the population of Morocco and Algeria and 60 percent of the populations of Tunisia and Libya are predominantly Berber by heredity. In contrast, in Egypt the historical roots of the population extend from the time of the Pharaohs; only 2 percent of the population has Berber roots. (Descendants of the ancient Egyptians are also not ethnically Arab, but, because they form the vast majority of the Egyptian population, issues involving ethnic origin are not as important in Egypt.)

Despite the Berbers' predominance in the ethnic heritage of the Maghreb, the term *Berber* (or *Amazigh*, in local usage) is now more commonly applied to rural people who speak a Berber dialect rather than to urban dwellers who might be descendents of this group but have adopted Arabic as their primary language.[54] Based on this definition, about 37 percent of Morocco's population is considered Berber and 21 percent of Algeria's.[55] The division between poor, rural populations whose first language is not Arabic and the urbanized, Arabic-speaking majority has been a source of political tension in Algeria and Morocco, especially as Berbers have pressed for greater use of local languages in the media, education, and government. These interethnic tensions have intensified as Berbers have migrated to cities to look for jobs.

---

[53] For example, while Hizbullah is committed in principle to establishing an Islamic state, it has deferred pursuing that goal in light of demographic realities, i.e. Lebanon's significant non-Muslim population. Al-Sayyid Hassan Nasrallah writes, in his short autobiography, "[Establishing an Islamic state] requires a referendum in which 90 percent of the people vote for it. At that point, and in keeping with this notion and the reality of the situation, the establishment of an Islamic Republic in Lebanon is not possible at this time" ("al-Sīra al-Dhātiya [Autobiography]," *al-Mustaqbal al-Arabi*, September 2006, p. 118).

[54] Tore Kjeilen, "Berbers," *LookLex Encyclopaedia*, undated web page.

[55] Harff, 1993, p. 230.

There is little to suggest that these tensions will dissipate in the near future. Although, historically, Berbers have become part of the larger Arabic-speaking populations, the divisions of language, income, and the rural/urban divide will continue to stoke resentment within Berber communities, especially in those countries where discrimination and lack of opportunity are felt the strongest.

The Kurds are an Indo-European group that speaks a language related to Persian.[56] Because they inhabit a mountainous borderland area, they were left much to their own devices until the early 20th century. After the emergence of the new nation-states in the region following the dissolution of the Ottoman Empire, the Kurds found themselves divided among four different countries: Iran, Iraq, Syria, and Turkey. Efforts by these nations to control this region and, by extension, to subsume Kurds into a new national identity resulted in resistance and frequent revolts. This history has created a strong sense of Kurdish identity and a mistrust of the governments in the region.

The Kurds are Iraq's largest ethnic minority, numbering 4 million to 5 million, or 15 to 20 percent of Iraq's total population. Between 2003 and 2007, when conflict intensified in Sunni Arab and mixed Sunni-Shi'a areas of Iraq, the Kurdish governorates were the most stable and prosperous in the country. However, disputes over the nature of Iraqi federalism and the distribution of oil revenues, particularly in the area around Kirkuk, have contributed to a rise in sectarian tensions.[57]

In addition to the Kurdish community, roughly 5 percent of Iraq's population consists of Turkomans, Assyrians, and other minorities.[58] Like the Kurds, Turkomans and Assyrians are also concentrated in the north, in the cities of Mosul and Kirkuk and the surrounding environs. However, rather than making common cause with the Kurds in pursuit of more autonomy, the existence of these other minorities in that region has added to the volatility in these areas.

The history of the region is replete with efforts by both local and international actors to exploit the Kurdish issue to gain an advantage in interstate conflicts. This has often taken the form of outside actors offering themselves as patrons to one of the Kurdish factions to gain leverage in pressing a separate agenda. At other times, the four states that are home to the Kurds—Iran, Iraq, Syria, and Turkey—have joined together to put down Kurdish attempts seeking autonomy. Because of the presence of U.S. forces in Iraq and the perception on the part of the Kurdish leadership of significant shared interests with Washington, the Iraqi Kurdish leadership finds the current situation favorable. As U.S. forces draw down and the security forces of the central government of Iraq become more proficient, Iraqi Kurds are likely to lose some of their current autonomy.

Although the approximately 1.7 million Kurds in Syria are also the largest ethnic minority group in that country, they form a smaller share of the population, less than 9.7 percent, than they do in Iraq.[59] In part because of their smaller numbers, the Syrian Kurds have been more quiescent than their counterparts in Iraq and Turkey. Divisions in Syria run more on confessional lines. Members of Syria's Alaouite minority run the country, even though three-

---

[56] Kamaran Kakel, "Who Are the Kurds?" undated web page.

[57] International Crisis Group, *Iraq and the Kurds: Resolving the Kirkuk Crisis*, Middle East Report 64, April 19, 2007.

[58] CIA, 2008.

[59] CIA, 2008.

quarters of the population is Sunni. A change in regime in Syria is likely to be characterized by Sunni religious leaders insisting that the Sunni majority gain a corresponding voice in governing the country; it is not clear whether the Kurds would also obtain a greater voice.

The Future

The Arab world is experiencing the same downward trends in fertility and population growth as is characteristic of Asia and Latin America, although somewhat later. As a consequence, pressures for public services will be shifting from rapidly adding new schools and providing health care to infants and children to a greater emphasis on secondary and higher education and health care for adults, especially treatment of chronic diseases of the elderly, such as diabetes, heart disease, and cancer.

Because of the large increases in population in the 1980s and 1990s, the numbers of young people entering the labor markets of these countries has been rising rapidly. In the wealthier Arab states, traditional measures to address demands for employment by expanding the government workforce will no longer suffice. In the poorer Arab countries, young adults are becoming increasingly dissatisfied with prospects in the informal economy. As the labor supply continues to expand rapidly for the next decade, young people will face continued difficulties in finding employment that meets their expectations.

The Arab world will become increasingly Muslim. The dwindling of non-Muslim religious communities in the Arab states makes the argument for a secular state that much more difficult to advance. However, secular influences in the form of more female participation in education and the labor force and through movies and television, Western and Arab alike, will accelerate ongoing changes in the role of women in society, acceptable social behavior, and differing interpretations of Islam.

The Energy Rich: A Second Chance

Introduction

The Arab economies, particularly those of the Persian Gulf states, are indelibly linked to energy. Of the 18 countries or entities we cover in this report, 13 produce oil or gas. Offshore discoveries in the Mediterranean could make Gaza and Lebanon natural producers as well. Of the current producers, we classify nine—Algeria, Bahrain, Iraq, Kuwait, Libya, Oman, Qatar, Saudi Arabia, and the UAE—as the "energy rich," countries for which energy exports constitute half or more of total exports of goods and services, for which energy contributes one-third or more of GDP, and that have a per capita income at PPP rates of at least $3,200 in 2005 dollars.

In this chapter, we first review the current role of the Arab world in global oil production and evaluate the region's likely future role. We then turn to an analysis of the economic performance of the energy-rich countries from the glory years of the 1970s through 2009, the consequences of poor economic policies for economic growth in the region, and the prospects for future economic growth with and in the absence of economic policy changes. We conclude with a discussion of the labor markets of the energy-rich countries.

When we examine the energy-rich countries in our study, we find the following:

- The Arab region is the world's most important source of oil, holds more than half of the world's proven reserves, and will not run into binding geological constraints on increasing oil output for decades.
- After a difficult two decades in the 1980s and 1990s, oil output rose 11 percent for the Arab Organization of the Petroleum Exporting Countries (OPEC) producers as a whole between 2000 and 2007 during a period of rising prices. Since prices hit historic peaks in 2008, they have slipped back but are still at relatively high levels compared to the previous decade.
- In the future, the combination of higher or stable output and higher prices will give the energy-rich countries a solid financial base. But projected increases in Arab oil output are not foreordained; they depend on whether the governments in the region choose to make the necessary investments and to produce at the levels projected by the Energy Information Administration (EIA).
- The economies of the energy-rich countries have experienced a wild ride over the past five decades, with per capita GDPs hit hard from 1980 through 2000 because of cutbacks in oil production, very large swings in the world market price of oil, and rapid population growth.

- Lackluster growth in per capita GDP following the 1970s, despite massive investments in infrastructure, factories, and education, was due to weak performance in terms of factor productivity. Poor government microeconomic policies that have distorted prices and impeded the formation and operation of private businesses have been a primary reason capital and labor have been used inefficiently.
- Although energy will continue to provide a ready source of revenues for governments in the future, the key to increasing per capita incomes will be rectifying the poor performance in improving factor productivity.
- During the heyday of energy boom, there was a staggering increase in demand for labor, local and foreign, followed by an exodus of foreign workers and declines in real public-sector wages during the more-difficult economic times of the 1980s and 1990s.
- Youth in many of the energy rich are dissatisfied with employment opportunities. Government employment and policies have discouraged the private sector from hiring or, if it hires, jobs in the richer states are often filled by foreign workers.

We discuss these findings in more detail in the remainder of this chapter.

Oil Production and Reserves of Energy-Rich Countries

The Present and Past

The Arab region is the world's most important source of oil, accounting for 32 percent of global production in 2008 (Figure 3.1). Of the countries in the region, Saudi Arabia is the largest oil producer in the world. In 2008, it pumped 10.8 million barrels per day (MBD) of oil and natu-

Figure 3.1
World Oil Production, 2008

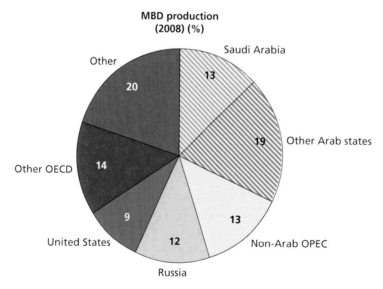

SOURCE: Energy Information Administration, "World Production of Crude Oil, NGPL, and Other Liquids, and Refinery Processing Gain, Most Recent Annual Estimates, 1980–2007," December 19, 2008.
NOTE: OECD = Organisation for Economic Co-Operation and Development.
RAND TR912-3.1

ral gas liquids, 13 percent of the world total, and 41 percent of output from the Arab world. Iraq, Kuwait, the UAE, and Algeria and Libya (in North Africa) are also major producers, pumping 1.9 MBD or more.

Not only are the Arab states the world's largest producers of oil; they also hold 55 percent of the world's proven reserves (Figure 3.2). Of total global reserves, Saudi Arabia accounts for 22 percent, and Iraq and the UAE account for 8 to 10 percent, respectively. Some recent estimates ascribe even larger reserves to Iraq. In addition to owning most of the world's reserves, the Persian Gulf is the only region in the world where new production can be developed rapidly and cheaply. Geology in Saudi Arabia, the other Gulf states, and Iraq is highly favorable, and drilling costs are relatively low. Oil is easily extracted, and the infrastructure to collect and ship oil is already in place. Production costs are among the lowest in the world.[1]

Some industry experts have argued that Saudi fields are being depleted more rapidly than thought, that development costs of new fields will be higher than expected, and that proven reserve estimates are too high.[2] Saudi Aramco, the national oil company, has rebutted these contentions, stating that it will be able to develop new fields and increase output without difficulty.[3] Of the two contentions, Saudi Aramco's is the more convincing. Even if rates of depletion are higher than previously estimated and production costs in the Persian Gulf double or triple estimates of a few dollars per barrel,[4] the Gulf states would remain the world's lowest-cost

Figure 3.2
Composition of World Oil Reserves

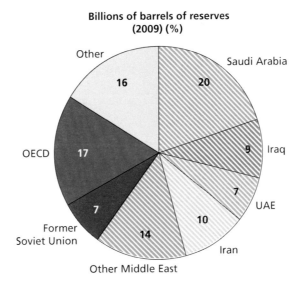

SOURCE: EIA, "International Energy Statistics," undated web page.
RAND *TR912-3.2*

---

[1]   EIA, 2004, p. 35.

[2]   Jeff Gerth, "Forecast of Rising Oil Demand Challenges Tired Saudi Fields," *New York Times*, February 24, 2004.

[3]   Mahmoud M. Abdul Baqi and Nansen G. Saleri, "Fifty-Year Crude Oil Supply Scenarios: Saudi Aramco's Perspective," Washington, D.C.: Center for Strategic and International Studies, February 24, 2004.

[4]   EIA, 2004, p. 37.

producers. The Gulf states will not run into binding geological constraints on increasing oil output for decades.[5]

The interests of all the Arab states are not the same when it comes to oil prices. Five generally smaller producers do not even belong to OPEC: Egypt, Oman, Syria, Tunisia, and Yemen. Their decisions not to join OPEC appear to have been driven by the desire to be free to pump, not just because they are not major producers; Qatar, a member of OPEC, does not produce much more oil than Oman. All five countries are poorer than the Gulf state members of OPEC. Although they generally have more-diversified economies than the richer Gulf states—oil is only one of several commodities that they export—oil revenues are important for their budgets. The governments of these states do not wish to have their production (and revenue) decisions tied to an organization in which they would have a very small voice.

OPEC members are frequently divided between price moderates and price hawks, with Arab members falling into both camps. Saudi Arabia and Kuwait have been considered price moderates, although Saudi Arabia has been more receptive to production cuts to prop up prices in recent years. Neither country is averse to high oil prices as long as prices are sustainable. But based on their past experiences, they find that extended periods of high oil prices have unpleasant consequences for OPEC. When prices are high, consumers invest in energy-saving machinery and equipment, such as more–fuel-efficient cars and trucks, and adjust their behavior to reduce consumption. High prices also have been followed by the development of competing sources of supply and a shift from oil to other fuels. Saudi Arabia and Kuwait do not wish to repeat the experience of the 1980s, when higher oil prices at the beginning of the decade led to a collapse in demand, as major consuming countries rapidly improved energy efficiency. They believe that it is in their countries' economic interest to keep oil prices within a range that does not encourage conservation or the development of more-expensive, non-OPEC fields or alternative fuels, such as coal-to-liquids or oil shale.[6] They already face competition from Canadian oil sands, which have become an important source of petroleum products.

OPEC members with smaller reserves or pressing needs for export revenues have often pushed for higher prices. As Saudi Arabia has been the swing producer, the cutbacks in production needed to sustain higher prices have primarily fallen on the Saudis and, to a lesser extent, on Kuwait, especially as the smaller producers frequently cheat on their assigned quotas, pumping and selling more than permitted under their agreements with the other OPEC members.[7] Not surprisingly, Saudi Arabia and Kuwait often take a jaundiced view of other members' pleas to increase prices through production cutbacks because these two countries carry most of the burden.

After a long lull in the 1980s and 1990s, Arab oil production has been on the upswing since 1998. Although the Arab states have accounted for the largest share of world oil production for a number of decades, their heyday was the 1970s. During that decade, production was rising—in some cases, very sharply—in four of the major producers (Algeria, Iraq, Saudi Arabia, and the UAE) at a time when prices were soaring (Figure 3.3). The 1970s were good even for such producers as Kuwait and Libya, where production fell because higher revenue from price increases more than compensated for drops in output. In contrast, the 1980s were

---

[5]   EIA, 2004, p. 37.

[6]   EIA, 2004, p. 27.

[7]   "OPEC Members' Cheating on Quotas Increases," *Bloomberg News*, January 19, 2010.

Figure 3.3
Oil Production of Major Arab Producers

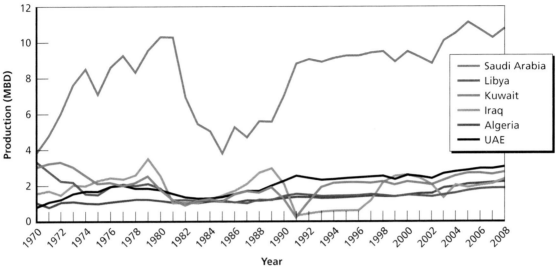

SOURCE: EIA, 2008.

RAND *TR912-3.3*

a difficult period, especially in the Persian Gulf. Oil output in Saudi Arabia more than halved, and Kuwait continued to cut production as these two producers supported prices by reducing exports. Iraqi exports and hence production were constrained by export access during the early period of the Iran-Iraq War, when the Iranians blockaded Um Qasr, Iraq's major port. Libyan production was falling in part because the state-owned company, created by Col. Muammar Abu Minyar al-Qadhafi from the foreign concessions he nationalized, was unable to sustain production on its own without foreign technical assistance.

The 1990s were a period of fluctuating prices as well as output (Figure 3.3). The decade started on a low note as Iraq invaded Kuwait. Before retreating, Iraq lit 720 Kuwaiti oil wells on fire, stopping Kuwaiti production.[8] The UN trade embargo imposed on Iraq in 1990 in retaliation for the invasion resulted in a drop in Iraqi production from 2.9 MBD in 1989 to 0.3 MBD in 1991, a fall of almost 90 percent. Strong economic growth in the developing world in the 1990s, especially Asia, provided a new source of demand for oil. Middle Eastern producers—in particular, Saudi Arabia—expanded output, filling the gap left by trade sanctions on Iraq and the drop in Kuwaiti production immediately following the Gulf War. However, when East Asia fell into recession in 1997–1998, demand for oil fell sharply, as did prices, because Saudi Arabia was too slow or unwilling to cut back its production rapidly enough to stop the slide in prices.

Between 2002 and 2008, oil producers operated in a very favorable environment. The world economy was growing rapidly. Increasing demand for transportation, especially from China and India, coupled with reductions in underutilized oil production capacity, resulted in sharp increases in world market oil prices, which surpassed previous peaks in real terms in 2008 (Figure 3.4). Subsequently, the global recession and the consequent fall in demand for

---

[8]   Mort Rosenblum, "Kuwait After the Gulf War: A Painful Insecurity," *CBS News*, January 14, 2001.

Figure 3.4
Nominal and Real Oil Prices in the Persian Gulf

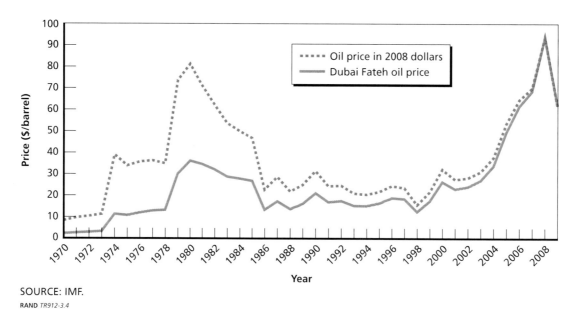

SOURCE: IMF.
RAND TR912-3.4

petroleum products resulted in a sharp fall in prices in the latter half of 2008 and 2009 (not shown in Figure 3.4).

Although producing oil at the prices of 2007 and early 2008 was very profitable, state-owned oil companies, especially those in the Gulf, were slow to expand capacity. Gulf governments remembered the sharp declines in world market oil prices when new production came on stream after the run-up in prices in the 1970s and did not want to contribute to a sharp fall in prices by rapidly expanding output.

The Future

After a difficult two decades in the 1980s and 1990s, the current decade has been kinder to oil producers, especially in the Persian Gulf. Output rose 11 percent for the Arab OPEC producers as a whole between 2000 and 2007; prices hit historic peaks. Every oil producer in the region, except Iraq, increased output during this period (Figure 3.5). Recently, Iraq has been increasing output as well.

The EIA projects that output of oil will continue to rise between 2007 and 2020, increasing 18 percent. However, more than half of the increase in output will be a result of the recovery in output in Iraq (Figure 3.5). As a whole, output is projected to grow just 1.3 percent per year. Prices are also projected to be strong. The combination of higher or more-stable output and higher prices will give the energy-rich countries a solid financial base.

Oil markets have been notoriously difficult to forecast, especially prices. However, even under low–oil-consumption scenarios, output from this region rises. Because the Arab states hold the largest share of world reserves and have the lowest development and extraction costs of any major oil-producing region in the world, slower-than-projected growth in demand results in slower-than-projected development of non-OPEC fields.[9]

---

[9]   EIA, *International Energy Outlook 2009*, DOE/EIA-0484(2009), May 27, 2009b, pp. 225–244.

Figure 3.5
Projected Oil Output from Selected Arab States

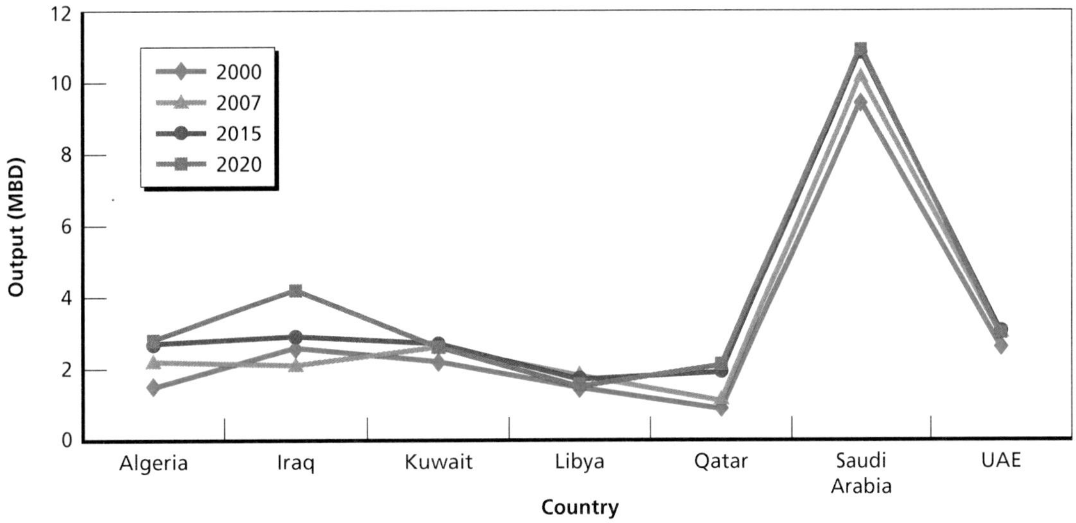

SOURCE: EIA, 2009b, p. 225.
RAND *TR912-3.5*

The projected increases in Arab oil output are not foreordained. They will depend on whether the governments in the region choose to make the necessary investments and to produce at the levels projected by the EIA. In light of the pressures the governments of these countries face to increase incomes of their citizens, these governments, especially those in the more-populous states, will seek to increase oil output. Recent shifts in attitudes toward foreign investment in national energy industries in Algeria, Kuwait, and Libya suggest that their governments have already decided to push for growth in capacity and output. However, political turmoil, reluctance to engage partners with the capital and expertise to accelerate development of domestic fields, or another upward surge in world market oil prices, which has eased current fiscal pressures, could all work to retard development of new fields.

In terms of future demand for oil and that demand's impact on the Arab world, since the large increases in world oil prices in the 1970s, the global economy has become much less energy dependent. Petroleum consumption per dollar of world GDP valued at PPP exchange rates fell by 46 percent between 1980 and 2006. During that period, petroleum consumption rose just 34 percent while global GDP rose 150 percent.

Despite forecasts of continued improvements in the efficiency with which the global economy uses petroleum over the next two decades, the EIA still projects that consumption of petroleum will rise at an average annual rate of 1.0 percent between 2010 and 2020, continuing at this rate through 2030.[10] Demand for transport—both personal and freight—and hence for refined oil products by the transport sector is expected to continue to grow strongly in developing countries, especially those in Asia.

Changes in technology, especially improvements in fuel economy in transportation, will help slow growth in demand but are unlikely to lead to a decline in consumption within the next two decades. The demand for oil is highly price inelastic: Even large increases in prices

---

[10] EIA, 2009b, p. 126.

have relatively little effect on amount demanded, at least in the short and medium terms. Alternative motor vehicle fuels, such as ethanol, natural gas, and biodiesel, remain expensive. Ethanol and biodiesel production faces capacity constraints because of the scarcity of land and competition from food crops. Although fuel economy is likely to improve, especially in the United States, overall growth in global demand is likely to swamp efficiency gains.

The EIA projects that the Arab world will account for about the same share of global oil production in 2020 (32.3 percent) as it did in 2008 (31.8 percent).[11] Arab oil production will be rising during a period when prices are likely to be high. According to our calculations, the value of Arab oil output in 2008 dollars surpassed its previous peak in 1980 in 2006. Despite the dip in prices in 2009, the EIA's base case in 2009 for oil prices assumed that oil prices would resume their upward climb, rising to $110 in 2008 dollars in 2015 and $130 in 2008 dollars in 2020. Even if these price increases do not transpire, small increases in production and exports, coupled with relatively high prices, will lead to very sizable earnings. In 2020, the value of production in the Arab states could total $1.34 trillion, more than six times their level in 1990 (Figure 3.6). In 2020, Arab producers will remain the dominant players in the oil market: the only producers with the extra capacity to increase output during times of rising prices or the financial reserves to reduce output if prices fall to levels lower than desired.

Despite the increases in value in this production, on a per capita basis, the increase in oil output and hence revenues will not return the major producers to the peaks of the late 1970s and early 1980s. For Saudi Arabia and Libya, per capita levels of oil revenues in 2020 are projected to run half their levels of 1980 in constant-dollar terms. For these countries, increases in oil output and higher prices will provide a respite from the declining trends in output and

Figure 3.6
The Value of Oil Production in the Arab States

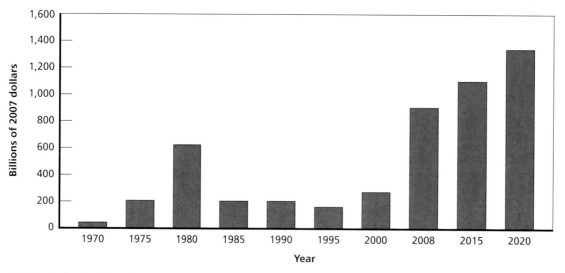

SOURCES: Historical data for prices come from IMF; data for production come from EIA. Forecasts are calculated from price forecasts from EIA, *Annual Energy Outlook 2009*, DOE/EIA-0383(2009), March 2009a, and production forecasts from EIA, 2009b.
RAND *TR912-3.6*

---

[11] EIA, 2009a, p. 126.

export revenues in the late 1980s and 1990s, but they will not restore per capita export revenues to the heady days of 1979 and 1980.

Economic Performance of Energy-Rich Countries

Among the energy rich, Saudi Arabia has the largest economy; in fact, it has the largest economy in the Arab world. Algeria, with a population one-third greater than Saudi Arabia's, has an economy one-third the size. The other economies vary from Bahrain, with a GDP of $2.2 billion, to the UAE, which had a GDP of $199 billion in 2007, more than twice the size of Morocco's, despite a population just 2 percent of Morocco's.

The economies of the energy-rich countries have experienced a wild ride over the past five decades. Many of the countries were dirt poor in the 1960s. In the early 1960s, Libya's primary export was scrap metal salvaged from the battlefields of World War II.[12] In the Gulf, the development of the oil fields and rising world demand for refined oil products in the 1960s contributed to very rapid rates of growth: During the 1960s, growth in per capita GDP in the Arab world was the highest among all the regions in the world, averaging 4.6 percent per year.[13] As a consequence, per capita GDP had already risen sharply before the first oil price rise in 1973. It continued to rise in the 1970s as oil prices rose. By 1980, the smaller Persian Gulf producers were fabulously wealthy, with per capita GDPs far exceeding that of the United States today. But by 1989, following the oil bust, per capita GDP had fallen back to or below its 1973 level in most of the countries (Figure 3.7). Since 1990, incomes have been rising again, especially in this decade, but, even by 2005, per capita incomes had still not recovered to their 1980 levels except in Bahrain and Oman, although Kuwait and Qatar were close.

Outside of the smaller Persian Gulf states, none of the larger energy-rich countries can be considered truly wealthy. As measured by per capita GDP, Algeria and Iraq have fallen back into the ranks of the lower-middle-income developing countries. The Libyans also have developing-country status. Per capita incomes in Oman and Saudi Arabia are not high by developed-country standards.

In the 1980s and 1990s, per capita GDPs in the energy-rich countries were hit hard on three accounts. First, as shown earlier in Figure 3.3, the Persian Gulf states cut back oil production in the 1980s to support the world market price. Because oil figures so large in their economies, the reduction in oil output resulted in sharp declines in GDP.

Second, the very large swings in the world market price of oil have had an enormous impact on the purchasing power of these countries: When oil prices rise, their terms of trade improve, with these countries being able to afford to purchase more imports because import prices have not risen commensurately. When oil prices fall, the ability to purchase imports declines. The decline in terms of trade in the 1980s, as the price of oil relative to import prices

---

[12] "[Early 1950s] Libya has been regarded by Westerners as not much more than a useless tract of desert. Its main exports were ones they could largely do without" (Mark Johnson, "Libyan Arab Jamahiriya," *New Internationalist*, No. 177, November 1987).

[13] Dipak Das Gupta, Jennifer Keller, and T. G. Srinivasan, *Reform and Elusive Growth in the Middle East: What Has Happened in the 1990s?* Washington, D.C.: World Bank, Human Development Group, Middle East and North Africa Region, working paper 25, June 2002, p. 17.

Figure 3.7
Per Capita GDP in Oil-Exporting Countries, 2005 Dollars

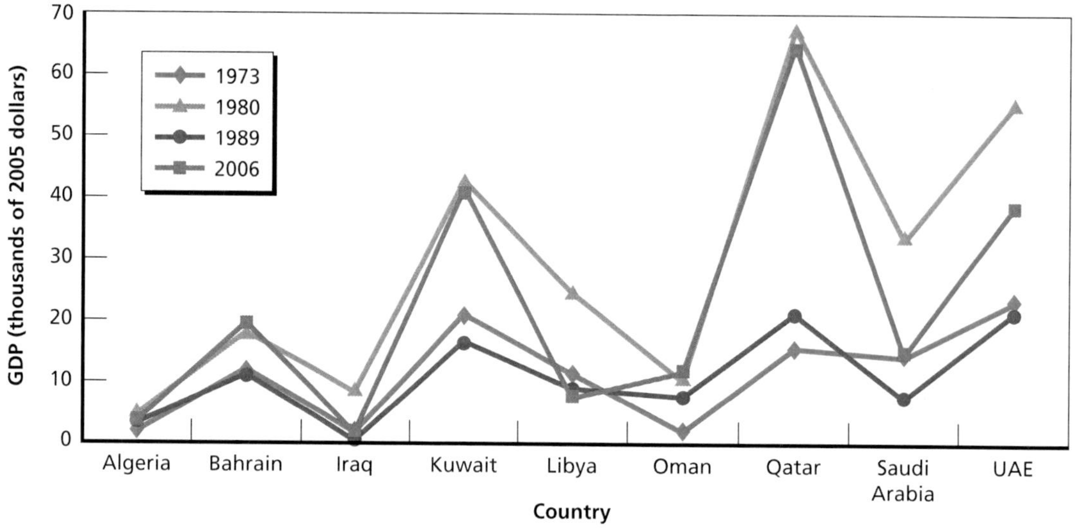

SOURCES: IMF; U.S. Census Bureau.
NOTE: Data for Bahrain and Libya are for 2005. The choice of dates was dictated by data availability and
international events. The first data on real GDP available for Bahrain were only from 1975. There were no
data available for Kuwait for 1990 and 1991 because of the economic consequences of the Gulf War.
RAND TR912-3.7

fell sharply, greatly reduced purchasing power and, hence, welfare. When oil prices rebounded,
these countries enjoyed the benefits of rising terms of trade again.

Third, populations grew rapidly over this period. Between 1972 and 2007, the populations of Algeria, Iraq, and Libya rose 2.4 to 2.7 times. Even in the Gulf states, where much of
the increase in population has been the result of an influx of foreign workers, rapid growth in
the indigenous populations has put pressure on the local governments to provide employment
opportunities and attempt to preserve incomes. The expanding population during a period of
declining oil revenues was the primary economic policy dilemma for the energy-rich states in
the 1990s. But even at the high oil prices of 2007 and 2008, the bigger countries divided a
pie that was smaller than in the 1970s among a much larger number of people. In 2009, this
problem worsened, especially for the poorer of the energy rich.

Figure 3.8 shows changes in per capita GDP in constant domestic prices. Because output
is valued in constant prices, changes in the world market price of oil do not directly intrude on
this series, although changes in oil prices do affect GDP in constant prices through their effects
on consumption and investment and associated sectors, such as retail trade and construction.
When oil prices are high, retail trade and construction boom; when they are low, output falls,
pulling down aggregate GDP. Nonetheless, this series does a better job of tracking trends in
output over the past decades than just looking at GDP in dollars.

The energy rich performed poorly between 1980 and 2000. In the 1980s, per capita GDP
plummeted in the Persian Gulf states. In the 1990s, most of the countries generated growth in
per capita GDP of less than 1 percent per year; in Saudi Arabia, per capita GDP actually fell.
Only Bahrain, Kuwait, and Qatar enjoyed appreciable growth.

Figure 3.8
Average Annual Changes in Per Capita GDP in Energy-Rich Countries

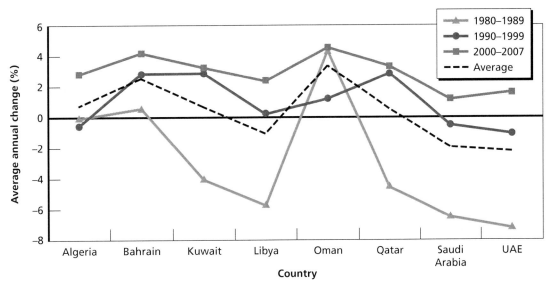

SOURCE: Calculated from IMF and U.S. Census Bureau data.
NOTE: Data for Bahrain and Qatar are for 1999–2005.
RAND *TR912-3.8*

The picture has noticeably improved in this decade largely because of higher prices for oil (Figure 3.8). However, lower prices for oil in 2009 and the global recession have slowed or, in the case of Dubai, put a halt to growth.

Why Did the Energy-Rich Economies Perform So Poorly Between 1980 and 2000?

In terms of trying to understand what has led to such poor performance in this period, we examine a number of potential causes, ranging from whether there is an "oil curse," the role of security in the region, and the supply of labor, capital, and factor productivity.[14]

An Oil Curse? The extraordinary increases in per capita incomes among the energy-rich states during the 1960s and 1970s created the impression, not least among the governments of these states, that oil wealth was a sure means of moving their countries from poverty to plenty. The poor economic performance of many of these countries between 1980 and 2000 moved the pendulum the other way. Some scholars have even argued that oil wealth is a "curse": They have found some evidence that countries with large endowments of natural resources tend to experience slower, more-erratic growth than countries that are not as well endowed with mineral resources.[15] In addition to slower and more-erratic growth, other scholars have found that states that are well endowed with energy and mineral wealth are less likely to be democratic.[16]

---

[14] For an excellent analysis of the reasons for disappointing growth in per capita incomes in the Arab states, see Marcus Noland and Howard Pack, *The Arab Economies in a Changing World*, Washington, D.C.: Peterson Institute for International Economics, April 2007.

[15] Jeffrey D. Sachs and Andrew M. Warner, "The Big Push, Natural Resource Booms and Growth," *Journal of Development Economics*, Vol. 59, No. 1, June 1999, pp. 43–76.

[16] Michael Lewin Ross, "Does Oil Hinder Democracy?" *World Politics*, Vol. 53, No. 3, April 2001, pp. 325–361.

Although these scholars find that oil wealth is correlated with slower growth and autocracy, none of the authors argues that mineral wealth is the only reason for poor economic performance. The influx of petrodollars has often led to poor allocation of resources and non-productive investments, but this outcome is not inevitable. A number of countries or states—e.g., Australia, Brazil, California, Malaysia, Mexico—have successfully used revenues from natural resources for public investments in education and infrastructure, creating a basis for strong, diversified growth. Then again, many other countries that are ruled by autocrats but are not energy rich have experienced slow growth or declines in per capita GDP. For example, Burkina Faso, Haiti, Niger, Paraguay, Sierra Leone, and Somalia are not well endowed in natural resources, but each has been subject to long periods of autocratic government and none has performed well economically. Oil wealth is one factor that can lead to poor investment decisions and an overreliance on energy as a source of income; however, this need not be the case.

We do not see stopping up the oil wells and halting energy exports as a productive strategy for accelerating growth in per capita GDP in the energy-rich countries. Oil curse or not, oil production, especially the value of oil production in constant dollars, continues to drive growth among the energy rich. As shown in Figure 3.9, oil still looms large in these economies: On average, energy accounts for half of GDP. Regressing GDP on oil production for these countries yields estimates suggesting that an increase in oil output leads to a more-than-commensurate increase in GDP: Oil production is an even more-important driver of growth than indicated by its share in GDP.[17]

Security. Not surprisingly, those energy rich that have been beset by war or insurgencies have suffered the economic consequences. Of the energy-rich countries, Algeria, Iraq, and Kuwait have suffered most from violence. In Algeria, after the Islamic Salvation Front (Front Islamique du Salut, or FIS), won the first round of national elections in December 1991, the army intervened to head off an Islamist victory. The abrogation of the results of the elections was followed by an active insurgency.[18] In the three years following the increase in violence, GDP fell 2.7 percent. In Kuwait, the scars of the Iraqi invasion affected the economy for more than a decade. In Iraq, wars, sanctions, and domestic insurgencies have wreaked havoc. Although the statistics are fraught with problems, in 2002, per capita GDP in constant dollars was estimated at one-eighth of its level in 1980. GDP fell an estimated 23 percent in 2003. Although security is considered a problem in almost all the energy-rich states, it has not yet had a measurable effect on GDP outside of these three countries.

Supply of Labor, Capital, and Factor Productivity. Stripped to its bare bones, GDP is often characterized as a function of labor, capital, and the productivity with which they are employed. Additional labor or capital coupled with increases in the productivity of these factors of production generates more output. In the case of energy-rich countries, it is also useful to throw endowments of natural resources into the pot. Discoveries of deposits of natural

---

[17] We regressed the log of an index for GDP for the 1970–2005 period on the log of an index for oil production for Algeria, Kuwait, Libya, Oman, Qatar, Saudi Arabia, and the UAE. Both GDP and oil output were set to 100 for the year 2000. The regression yielded the following parameters: $\ln(GDP) = 1.06 + 0.74 \times \ln(oil)$. The F-statistic was 107, and T-statistics were 6.2, 9.3 and 13.6, respectively; N = 239, and adjusted R-squared was 0.61. When we substituted an index for the value of oil in constant-priced dollars, the parameter on the oil variable fell to 0.46. We also employed a specification incorporating a time trend. That regression yielded the following parameters: $\ln(GDP) = 1.48 + 0.53 \times \ln(oil) + 0.028 \times time$. The F-statistic was 188, and T-statistics were 3.35 and 10.3, respectively; N = 239, and adjusted R-squared was 0.61. In this instance, we substituted an index for the value of oil in constant-priced dollars; the results were virtually the same.

[18] Lisa Ficklin, "The Groupes Islamistes Armées (GIA)," Islamic Institute for Human Rights, date unknown.

Figure 3.9
Role of Energy in the Economies of the Energy Rich

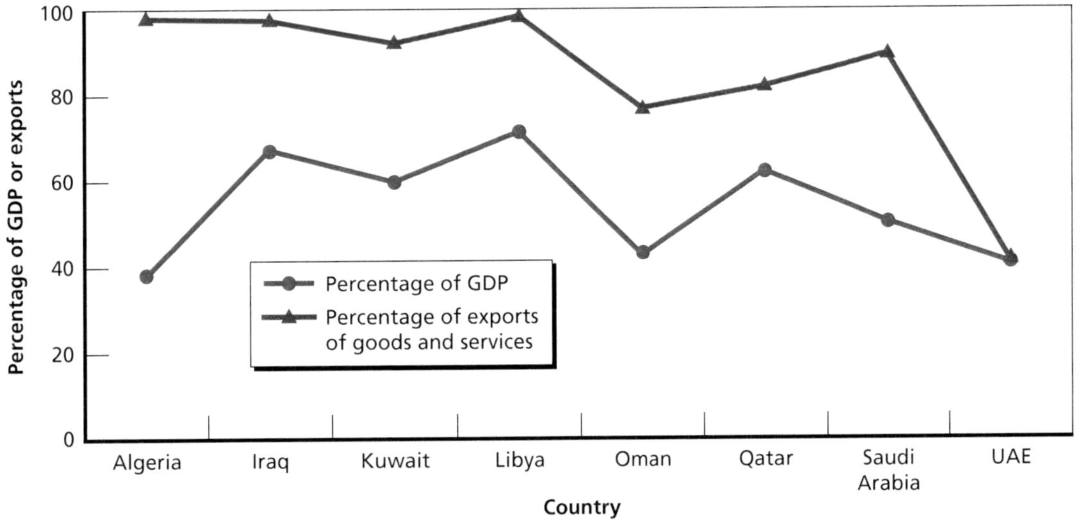

SOURCES: Data from IMF and the Planning Council, State of Qatar.
NOTE: Data on the role of energy in GDP and exports were available for only certain years. These data were
for the following years: Algeria, 2004; Iraq, 2004; Kuwait, 2005 (GDP), 2004 (exports); Libya, 2005; Oman, 2002;
Qatar, 2004; Saudi Arabia, 2005 (GDP), 2004 (exports); and Yemen, 2003.
RAND TR912-3.9

resources create an additional source of economic growth. However, once discovered, capital and labor are needed to develop endowments of natural resources, so capital and labor remain key inputs into the production process. Thus, changes in the supply of labor and capital and in factor productivity remain the best places to begin analyzing the economic performance of these countries.

Labor. The supply of labor has not placed a binding constraint on economic growth in these countries. As noted in Chapter Two, rapid population growth has resulted in a substantial influx of young people into the labor market. In Algeria, the labor force has been growing by 3.1 percent per year, even as the increase in population has fallen to 1.5 percent per year.[19] The high priority that governments of the energy-rich countries have given education since the 1960s has led to an increase in human capital in addition to the expansion of the labor force.

During boom years in the wealthier countries among the energy rich, businesses and government agencies recruit labor from abroad if the supply of local workers is inadequate. Many of the energy rich have hired doctors, teachers, engineers, and other professionals to staff and manage rapidly growing activities in these sectors. They have also hired hundreds of thousands of less skilled foreign laborers to staff stores, provide child care and other household services, and provide workers for construction projects. Energy-poor Arab states have often been major suppliers, although South Asia is the most important source of labor for the Gulf states. Thus, the supply of labor in these countries has not been a major problem: Where skill shortages exist, the energy-rich countries have well-developed mechanisms for attracting expatriate staff.

---

[19] Khanjar Wabel Abdallah, Philippe Callier, Taline Koranchelian, and Michael Lazare, *Algeria: Selected Issues and Statistical Appendix*, Washington, D.C.: International Monetary Fund, country report 03.69, February 7, 2003, p. 3.

A bigger problem has been how to induce businesses to employ indigenous labor rather than foreign workers, even in poor countries, such as Iraq.

Capital. During the 1970s and early 1980s, the explosion in oil revenues permitted governments to invest heavily. In dollar terms, between 1970 and 1978, investment rose eightfold in Algeria and 39 times in Saudi Arabia. During this period, construction was more-often constrained by the availability of cement and the time needed to plan and complete projects than by the ability to finance them. Investment was so strong that, between 1970 and 1980, the physical stock of capital per worker in the Arab states rose by 60 percent.[20] Governments not only invested in public infrastructure; they also chose to invest, often heavily, in capital-intensive industries, such as cement, refineries, and petrochemicals. Private firms and individuals invested in real estate and housing. This boom is being replicated in this decade, as high oil prices contributed to a massive building boom in the Gulf states and, to a lesser extent, Libya.

The collapse in oil prices in the mid-1980s was followed by a collapse in investment as well. After peaking in Algeria and Saudi Arabia in 1978 at 48.5 and 30.7 percent of GDP, respectively, by 1990, the share of investment in GDP had halved in both countries. However, the investments of the 1970s and early 1980s left a legacy of nationwide systems for electric power, telecommunications, water, and sewage. The energy-rich countries of the Arab world are generally better endowed with physical capital than other developing countries with similar per capita GDPs.

Factor Productivity. Despite massive investments in infrastructure, factories, and education, the energy-rich countries of the region have not used labor or capital well. The investments in human and physical capital have failed to pay off in terms of accelerated growth in per capita GDP; they have been accompanied by a decline in the efficiency with which these inputs are used. According to Abdallah et al., total factor productivity for the Arab countries as a whole *declined* by 1.4 percent per year in the 1970s when improvements in human capital are taken into account. This decline persisted into the 1980s, running 1.3 percent per year.[21] The performance of the major energy-exporting countries was the worst in this regard. During the 1980s, total factor productivity declined by 5.1 percent per year in Saudi Arabia and 5.3 percent per year in Kuwait.[22] Although the changing price of oil and reductions in output of oil in the Gulf states had the most-immediate impact on the size of GDP, a major factor explaining the slow pace of economic growth and declines in per capita GDP in these countries between 1980 and 2000 has been the fall in factor productivity, especially the productivity of capital.

Why this poor performance in terms of factor productivity? Although mineral wealth appears to make it easier for governments to avoid difficult policy decisions—decisions that would improve economic performance—governments of energy-rich countries are not destined to pursue counterproductive economic policies. Bahrain and Oman, two smaller Persian Gulf energy exporters, have managed to outperform the larger countries in terms of economic growth during this period. There is a substantial body of research attesting to the importance of sensible macroeconomic policies and relatively efficient government institutions and regula-

---

[20] Das Gupta, Keller, and Srinivasan, 2002, p. 19.

[21] Abdallah et al., 2003, p. 20.

[22] Das Gupta, Keller, and Srinivasan, 2002, p. 30.

tory policies for increasing productivity.[23] In the next section, we examine each of these conditions in turn.

Monetary and Fiscal Policies. Inflation is the primary sign of imprudent macroeconomic policies. If the banking system is lending too profligately or the government fails to keep its budget balance under control, central banks might bail out these institutions by expanding the money supply. As the money supply rises, inflation accelerates.

Because of large earnings from energy exports and generally sensible fiscal policies, the Persian Gulf states have usually kept inflation firmly under control, although, during periods of rapid economic growth, inflation has sometimes accelerated, as was the case in 2007 and 2009 (Figure 3.10). In fact, the Gulf region has one of the better track records on inflation of any region in the world. After a period of rapid inflation in the 1990s, Algeria has also brought inflation down. Iraq registered inflation rates of between 200 and 500 percent between 1993 and 1995; still, after a surge following the invasion, inflation has subsided in Iraq as well.

With the partial exception of Iraq, poor macroeconomic policies do not explain declines in factor productivity and per capita GDP in these countries. Commendable performance on inflation is not foreordained for energy exporters. Nigeria and Venezuela have poor records. Despite substantial oil earnings, their governments have been unsuccessful at keeping government expenditures in check. The performance of the smaller Gulf states and, more recently, Algeria reflects more-disciplined approaches to budgetary expenditures or the ability to tap assets to finance expenditures. In Saudi Arabia, for example, large deficits in years of low oil

Figure 3.10
Average Annual Rates of Inflation in Energy-Rich Countries

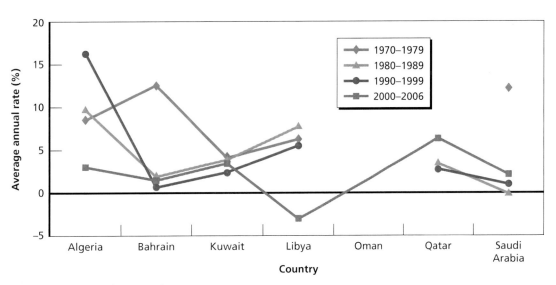

SOURCE: Calculated from IMF data.
NOTE: Data for Libya are through 2006.
RAND TR912-3.10

[23] For example, Paul Collier, *Breaking the Conflict Trap: Civil War and Development Policy*, Washington, D.C.: World Bank, 2003; Johannes Fedderke and Robert Klitgaard, "Economic Growth and Social Indicators: An Exploratory Analysis," *Economic Development and Cultural Change*, Vol. 46, No. 3, April 1998, pp. 455–489; and Daniel Kaufmann and Aart Kraay, "Governance and Growth: Causality Which Way? Evidence for the World, in Brief," Washington, D.C.: World Bank, February 2003.

prices have been financed by running down reserves and later by borrowing from their own banks and social insurance fund, not by printing money. Inflationary problems in 2007 and 2008 in Kuwait, Qatar, Saudi Arabia, and the UAE stemmed from exchange rate policies rather than loose fiscal policies. Because these countries peg their currencies against the dollar, when the dollar falls against other major currencies, these countries import inflation as the cost of imports in euros and other stronger currencies rise. Supply-side rigidities in local markets, especially for real estate, have also served to accelerate inflation rates.

Microeconomic Policies. The primary reason for declines in factor productivity in the energy-rich Arab countries has been poor microeconomic policies: government policies that have distorted prices and impeded the formation and operation of private businesses. Even in the case of Iraq, poor microeconomic policies have exacerbated the economic damage caused by war and sanctions.

Prices are the signals that drive economic change. On the demand side, increases in prices discourage consumption, encouraging consumers to change their consumption patterns. On the supply side, price increases encourage producers to expand production or enter new markets. If prices do not reflect costs of production or changes in demand, they fail to provide the necessary signals for consumers and producers to respond in a manner that leads to economic growth.

Ease of entry into new markets and the bureaucratic costs of doing business are key factors in eliciting supply-side responses. When businesses can easily enter promising markets, competitive pressures more quickly lead to increases in supply and the reallocation of resources to the production of goods and services that are in greater demand. When producers are inhibited from entering new markets or expanding their activities, new supplies of goods and services fail to make their way to markets.

In most of the Arab world, including the energy-rich countries, governments have intervened heavily in markets by imposing price controls, providing subsidies, and erecting barriers to entry and trade. Price controls and subsidies have been adopted to curry favor with the populace. Bureaucrats have erected barriers to entry and raised the operating costs of businesses in response to government preferences and to better request bribes. In some countries, leaders of the local business community have pushed to prevent new entrants from emerging to compete with them. It is these measures that have served to distort the allocation of labor and capital away from more-efficient uses. As factor productivity growth is, by definition, improvements in the efficiency with which factors of production are used, government policies in the Arab world that distort prices and market signals are the most-suspect causes of poor performance in terms of growth in factor productivity.

Price Controls and Subsidies. Each of the energy-rich countries of the region provides subsidies or imposes price controls on politically sensitive products. Price controls on energy are endemic. Retail prices of gasoline have generally been held below wholesale (export) prices in the Persian Gulf: Governments force the national oil companies to absorb the difference as a loss.[24] In addition, all the governments of the energy-rich states have sold electricity at subsidized prices or, in some cases, given it away for free to favored industrial users and households.[25]

---

[24] As of February 2008, retail prices per gallon of gasoline ran $0.93 in Iraq, $0.78 in Kuwait, $0.45 in Saudi Arabia, and $0.85 in the UAE. Wholesale gasoline prices ran $2.35 per gallon.

[25] For example, Saudi Arabia subsidized half of the cost of electric power to rural inhabitants (Kiren Aziz Chaudhry, *The Price of Wealth: Economies and Institutions in the Middle East*, Ithaca, N.Y.: Cornell University Press, 1997, p. 152).

Price subsidies for water and inflated prices for agricultural products have encouraged overconsumption of water. During the 1980s, Saudi Arabia became an exporter of wheat as the government paid farmers prices for wheat that were, at times, almost nine times world market prices.[26] As a consequence, Saudi businesses drilled wells to pump water from ancient aquifers to grow wheat in the desert that the Saudi government eventually dumped on world markets at a loss.[27] The increased demand for water for agricultural use in Saudi Arabia has resulted in overexploitation of aquifers, forcing the government to make additional investments in desalinization plants. Only in 2008 did the government finally announce that subsidies will be phased out by 2016,[28] because the depletion of "fossil water" aquifers has reached a point at which it endangers the provision of water for human consumption. In Iraq, agricultural demand for water for which there is no charge has led to overinvestment in irrigation systems and overutilization of water from rivers. The additional agricultural production made possible by these investments has not been enough to provide an adequate rate of return for the cost of constructing these facilities.

These price controls and subsidies and the ensuing price distortions are a major reason for the declining productivity of capital among the energy rich. When domestic prices differ markedly from prices on world markets, producers and consumers receive the wrong signals. Producers are encouraged to use scarce resources to produce products that can be more efficiently and cheaply imported, such as wheat in Saudi Arabia. Price controls on refined oil products have led to heavy investments in refining capacity undertaken to satisfy artificially induced demand. These investments, made in response to distorted signals sent by price controls and subsidies, have had low or negative rates of return. They have been an important cause of the decline in the productivity of capital in these countries.

Governments in the region have argued that subsidies and price controls are necessary to diversify their economies, weaning them from their dependence on oil and natural gas. However, these policies have done the reverse. If production generates losses, these losses have to be covered by profitable economic activities, e.g., the production of oil and gas. To the extent that production of nonoil goods and services is dependent on subsidies or price controls on energy to be viable, the economies have become more, rather than less, dependent on energy or revenues from energy exports for the generation of GDP.

Barriers to Entry. Differences in official attitudes in the region toward the private sector are striking: From independence until the late 1980s, Algerian governments drew up national economic plans and created and supported state-owned companies, explicitly and implicitly discriminating against the private sector.[29] In Libya, Qadhafi's philosophy of *jamahiriya*, propagated through his *Green Book*,[30] led to the imposition of numerous restrictions on private ownership and the operation of private businesses, including in the bazaars.[31] These strictures on private businesses have hindered economic growth in Algeria and Libya and reduced the

---

[26] Chaudhry, 1997, p. 183.

[27] Chaudhry, 1997, p. 183.

[28] "Saudi Scraps Wheat Growing to Save Water," *Middle East Online*, January 8, 2008.

[29] Michel Lazare, Philippe Callier, Khanjar Wabel Abdallah, and Taline Koranchelian, *Algeria: Selected Issues and Statistical Appendix*, International Monetary Fund, January 29, 2003, p. 7.

[30] Muammar Qaddafi, *Green Book*, unauthorized ed., Henry M. Christman, ed., Buffalo, N.Y.: Prometheus Books, 1988.

[31] IMF, 2003b.

productivity of labor and capital because the stunted private sector has not been able (or, in some cases, has been forbidden) to provide jobs that would better utilize available labor. Curbs on the private sector have also reduced capital productivity because investment has been channeled into state-owned enterprises that have squandered these resources; not surprisingly, private savings are frequently invested abroad.

In contrast, the Persian Gulf states have generally been supportive of private business: Many members of the royal families are entrepreneurs.[32] Despite these differences, barriers to entry in the Persian Gulf countries have also served to reduce factor productivity. Governments of the Persian Gulf states have used licensing and contracting to favor specific providers. Initially, some governments, such as Qatar, issued only one license for mobile telephone services. The company that obtained the license had a monopoly, reducing the provision of service so as to maintain higher prices than is the case in more-competitive markets. Foreign investors have faced discrimination and, in some instances, are barred from investing in certain designated sectors.

Government contracting procedures and administrative barriers to entry also foster corruption, further serving to reduce factor productivity. Although private businesses in Libya and, until recently, Algeria encountered more difficulty with licensing and registration procedures than in the Gulf states, bureaucratic barriers to entry exist in all the countries, retarding economic growth and the more-efficient use of labor and capital. For example, in Saudi Arabia, foreign companies can compete for government contracts only if they worked with a Saudi partner. Some businesses have resorted to bribes to circumvent these administrative barriers; some civil servants have sought to keep these barriers high or to increase the administrative costs of doing business so they can more easily extort these bribes.

According to Transparency International's Corruption Perceptions Index, Libya and Algeria score 126 and 92, respectively, out of 180 countries in terms of corruption.[33] According to foreign companies, the Gulf countries have reduced corruption in recent years. Saudi Arabia currently scores 80 in the world, but Oman, Qatar, and the UAE score well, ranking 41, 28, and 35, respectively, as shown in Figure 3.11.

Barriers to Trade. All the energy-rich states have relatively small economies, either because they are poor (Algeria and Iraq) or because they have small populations (most of the rest). Only Saudi Arabia can claim to have a medium-sized economy on a global scale, befitting its membership in the Group of Twenty (G-20). In light of the small sizes of their economies and the very marked comparative advantage they enjoy in the production of oil and natural gas, the gains these countries enjoy from engaging in trade are potentially very large.

Despite the potential for reaping gains from trade, a number of the energy exporters are protectionist. Algeria, Iraq, and Libya are only observers in the World Trade Organization (WTO). Saudi Arabia joined only in 2005. Algeria and Libya use a complex system of high tariffs, import licensing, and quotas to control imports. High tariffs on manufactured imports have made it difficult for Algerian entrepreneurs to import components for assembly and small-scale manufacturing operations, stymieing the growth of these activities. Libya and, to a lesser extent, Algeria have employed multitier exchange rate schemes to channel trade, with one rate for the private sector and another for state-owned enterprises.

---

[32] Chaudhry, 1997, p. 171.

[33] Johann Graf Lambsdorff, "Corruption Perceptions Index 2006," Transparency International, November 6, 2006; Johann Graf Lambsdorff, "Corruption Perceptions Index 2007," Transparency International, September 26, 2007.

Figure 3.11
Transparency International's Corruption Index for 2008

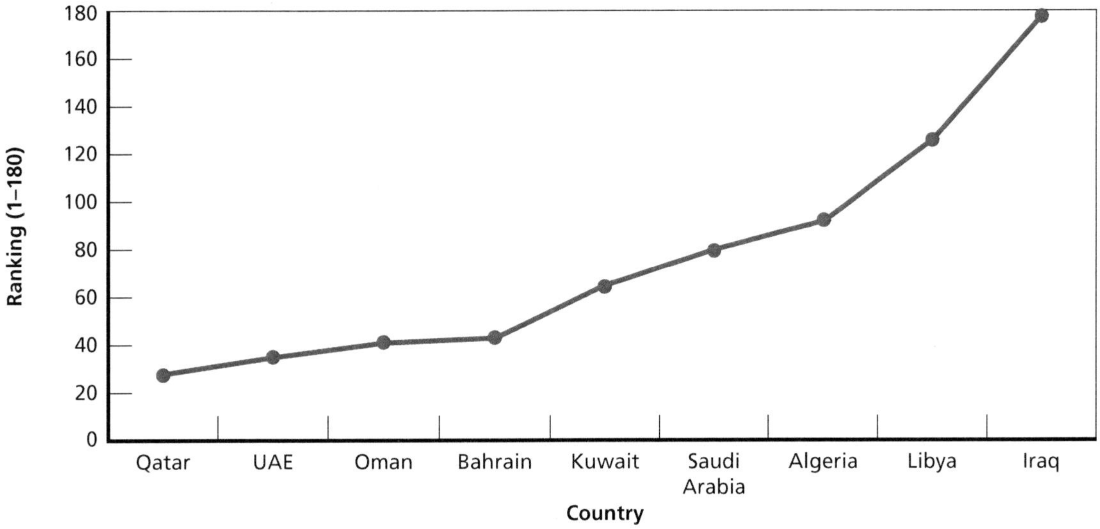

SOURCE: Johann Graf Lambsdorff, "Corruption Perceptions Index 2008," Transparency International, September 22, 2008.
RAND *TR912-3.11*

These systems distort decisions about importing and exporting, sending the wrong signals about what to produce and what not to produce, thereby reducing the efficiency with which capital and labor are employed. Exporters, forced to convert foreign currency earnings into domestic currency at the lower, less favorable official rate pay an implicit tax on their export earnings in the form of the difference between what they could receive selling foreign currency earned from exports at the free-market rate and the rate they receive from the government. Those importers blessed with access to foreign currency at the more-favorable official exchange rate benefit from an implicit subsidy. They are able to purchase items from abroad much more cheaply than competitors that have to purchase foreign currency at free-market rates. The welter of rules and regulations governments have to employ to prevent arbitrage—the sale of foreign currency purchased cheaply at the official rate at the much higher free-market rate—introduces another layer of administrative cost and inefficiencies.

The better-performing energy exporters have attempted to carve out an alternative path. Tariffs in the Gulf states have been relatively low, although most governments have used subsidies for electricity, land, and water to enable domestic producers to compete against importers. Bahrain and the UAE—Dubai in particular—have adopted liberal trade policies that have made them regional shopping centers. These policies have contributed to rapid growth in retail and wholesale trade; transportation, including shipping and airlines; and trade finance, which has helped spur the growth of the financial sector. Free-trade zones have encouraged growth in manufacturing as well. The economic policies followed by the Gulf states show that more-open trading regimes can stimulate growth in nonenergy sectors.

State-Directed Investments and State-Owned Companies. All the governments of the energy-rich countries have used revenues from energy exports to embark on ambitious programs of investment and industrialization. The desire to "modernize" drove investments in power plants, roads, ports, housing, schools, water and sewage systems, and airports. Rate of return was frequently not a driving factor in sizing or deciding which of these investments to make.

Investment did not stop at infrastructure. All the countries created state-owned companies to drive industrialization, ranging from airlines to cement companies to petrochemical concerns. By creating these enterprises, the governments hoped to diversify their economies, creating a basis for growth not founded on exports of crude oil and natural gas. For a period, these companies and government bureaucracies became the most-important employers. They remain important components of the economy and are a major reason for the declines in factor productivity that these countries have suffered in the past few decades.

Government investments in state-owned entities outside energy have often gone to white elephants. These enterprises have been protected by high tariff barriers, formal and informal barriers to entry facing potentially competing firms, and government guarantees. Because they are major employers and sources of patronage, it is almost impossible to close them, for political reasons. Employees have enjoyed a virtual guarantee on their jobs. Managers face little encouragement to make tough decisions; in many instances, advancement is dictated by family ties (the Gulf states) or political patronage, not performance. Not surprisingly, these enterprises have become an enduring drain on the treasuries, slowing growth by sucking resources from potentially more-profitable uses.

In the Gulf states, state-owned investment banks readily provided loans for any and all projects put forward by local entrepreneurs. The banks lacked the ability or the desire to evaluate projects in terms of creditworthiness. In many instances, they were victims of, or complicit in, fraud, with credits designated for specific purposes, such as residential construction, used for other purposes. In some instances, borrowers took the money and ran. The banks made little effort to collect the loans.[34]

In this decade, the Gulf states have aggressively privatized a number of these formerly state-owned enterprises. Shares in state-owned telephone companies have been sold off in Oman, Qatar, and the UAE. Shares in manufacturing facilities, such as petrochemical and cement plants, have also been sold. In many instances, these semiprivatized companies still receive special treatment from the local governments, but they are beginning to face more competition and tougher operating conditions.

What Is the Outlook for Economic Growth in the Energy-Rich Countries?

The energy rich have not been immune from the global recession. The rich Gulf Cooperation Council (GCC) states have been hit hard by the fall in the price of oil and the collapse in value of their large stock of financial investments in the OECD states and the Gulf itself. At their nadir, Gulf equity markets had dropped 58 percent in value.[35] Despite these hits, countercyclical spending on the part of local governments and growth in nonoil sectors are projected to keep the group as a whole out of recession.[36] The World Bank projects a slight acceleration in growth in 2010 and return to trend-line growth of 4.5 percent per year in 2011.

Going forward, economic output, especially for the smaller Gulf states, will likely continue to be closely linked to oil output and prices because of the large role of oil and gas in

---

[34] Chaudhry, 1997, p. 237.

[35] World Bank, *Global Development Finance 2009: Charting a Global Recovery*, Washington, D.C., 2009, p. 127.

[36] World Bank, 2009, p. 128.

these economies. Even for the more-populous countries of Algeria and Iraq, oil and gas will likely loom large. However, oil and gas exports will serve more as a foundation rather than a driver of growth. As shown in Figure 3.5, only in Iraq are projected increases in oil production substantial. In the other countries, per capita output of oil falls. Even in Iraq, where oil output is projected to double, the substantial projected increases in oil output fail to enable the country to make up ground lost over the past quarter-century of economic decline. Consequently, although energy will continue to provide a ready source of revenues for governments, the key to increasing per capita incomes will be rectifying the poor performance of these countries in improving factor productivity.

Figure 3.12 compares potential growth in per capita GDP in the energy rich for 2010 to 2020 under two scenarios. In the first scenario, GDP is assumed to grow at the average rate enjoyed by the country between 2000 and 2008. In the second scenario, growth falls back to the rates of 1990 to 2000. In both scenarios, per capita GDP is calculated by dividing projected GDP by population as forecast by the U.S. Census Bureau. These are not predictions. The purpose of the exercise is to illustrate the difference in per capita incomes that a more-conducive environment for economic growth could make.

The differences for most of these countries are stark. If the economic environment is as conducive to growth in the next decade as it was between 2000 and 2008, per capita GDP will rise by 1.5 to 3 percent in the larger countries. Although unlikely, in this scenario, the smaller Gulf states would continue to enjoy extraordinarily high rates of growth in per capita GDP. However, if the economic environment in these countries returns to that of the 1990s, the larger energy-rich economies could face severe social pressures. At a time when labor forces in these countries are still growing rapidly, growth in per capita GDP would range from a decline of 0.4 percent per year for Libya to an increase of 1.3 percent in Saudi Arabia. In none of these countries would increases in output be substantial enough to provide tangible increases in

Figure 3.12
Change in Per Capita GDP in the Energy Rich Between 2010 and 2020 Using Average Growth Rates of the 1990s and from 2000 to 2008

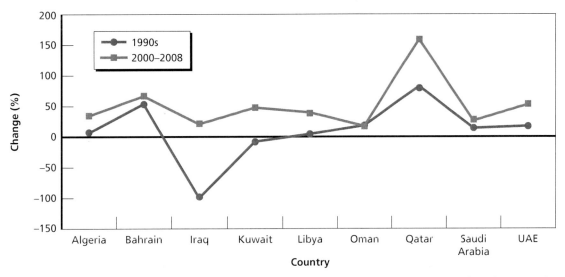

SOURCE: RAND calculations. GDP estimates for 2008 taken from IMF, *World Economic Outlook (WEO): Crisis and Recovery*, Washington, D.C., April 2009, pp. 193–195.
RAND *TR912-3.12*

average wages, especially if women participate more actively in the labor force. In contrast, the very high per capita incomes in the smaller Gulf states, coupled with the ability to reduce the size of the expatriate labor force, provide those governments with other instruments to preserve growth in per capita incomes for nationals.

Assuming that these countries will continue to preserve macroeconomic stability in a favorable international environment for energy producers, what else do they need to do to maintain favorable conditions for growth? First, these countries need to reduce price distortions by cutting producer and, to the extent politically feasible, consumer price subsidies.

Second, in the cases of Algeria and Libya, barriers to trade in the form of high, differentiated tariffs, quotas, multiple exchange rate systems, and import licenses need to be eliminated. Barriers to foreign investment ought to be reduced. For those countries that have not yet joined the WTO, membership would provide a useful discipline in this area. Continued expansion and integration of the GCC would do much to increase competition and improve factor productivity in member states.

Third, barriers to entry facing new businesses need to be dismantled. In Algeria and Libya, this can take the form of reducing administrative barriers, such as long, complicated registration procedures, punitive taxes on businesses, and complicated regulations that make it easy for the bureaucracy to request bribes. State-owned development banks have provided subsidized credits to enterprises that enjoy official favor. Charging these banks with maximizing long-term, risk-adjusted rates of return or investing oil revenues in private-sector investment funds or banks would result in substantial improvements in rates of return on investment and the efficiency with which capital is utilized. It would also provide a useful discipline to investment decisions by the enterprise sector while doing a better job of ensuring that the financial benefits of the countries' energy wealth extend to future generations. Privatization of non–energy-sector assets has improved efficiency and generated more-rapid growth in revenues and output of formerly state-owned enterprises in those Arab countries that have braved this step. A more-aggressive approach to privatization would generate additional benefits in terms of accelerated growth in factor productivity.

How likely are the governments of the energy-rich countries to adopt policies that would foster more-efficient use of resources? All show some signs of liberalizing economic policies. The GCC member states have lowered barriers to trade and entry, have already created a customs union, and are discussing the adoption of a common currency.[37] Algeria has taken significant strides toward liberalizing prices and reducing barriers to trade and entry for private businesses since the late 1980s.[38] More recently, Libya has also begun to take steps to liberalize its economy.[39] The Iraqi government has maintained much more-liberal economic policies than it had under Saddam Hussein. Going forward, we expect the GCC countries to continue to push ahead with economic liberalization, regional integration, and privatization. Because of their conservative fiscal policies, with the exception of Dubai, these governments have been able to weather the global recession better than most other regions in the world. If oil prices continue to stay substantially higher than their average levels of the 1990s, the citizens of the

---

[37] Ugo Fasano and Zubair Iqbal, "Common Currency," *Finance and Development*, Vol. 39, No. 4, December 2002.

[38] Lazare et al., 2003, p. 7.

[39] IMF, *The Socialist People's Libyan Arab Jamahiriya: 2003 Article IV Consultation—Staff Report, Staff Statement, Public Information Notice on the Executive Board Discussion*, country report 03/327, October 2003b, p. 4.

smaller countries should continue to enjoy high levels of incomes and continued growth. However, subsidies will remain a problem. Few of the Gulf states have seriously wrestled with the role of state subsidies in their economies.

In Algeria, Iraq, and Libya, the outlook for concerted economic liberalization is cloudier. After 15 years of moves to liberalize its economy, Algeria remains a corrupt state, with widespread restrictions on product and capital markets and an extraordinarily large, inefficient public sector. Libya's first steps toward liberalization have been tentative and have already provoked substantial opposition from within the government. Although the overriding determinant of economic growth in Iraq will be the security situation, if security does not deteriorate, economic policies will play a key role. The Iraqi government was bequeathed a fairly liberal economic environment and policies from the Coalition Provisional Authority and the transitional government, but the overwhelming levels of corruption in that country and the push on the part of Iraq's many political groups for a share of the country's oil wealth have slowed growth above and beyond the problems posed by the lack of security.

Finally, none of these countries has successfully addressed the issue of state employment. The more-pressing economic issue for these governments will be to devise incentives to encourage new entrants to the labor force to seek jobs outside of government. Modest shifts in expectations have taken place in some of these countries, as jobs in private finance and some service industries have become socially acceptable, but the government overwhelmingly remains the preferred employer. In light of these political difficulties, we are cautiously optimistic that these regimes will continue to pursue more-rational economic policies, but we do not expect them either to cut employment of nationals in overstaffed state bureaucracies or state-controlled companies or to eliminate subsidies.

Labor Markets of the Energy-Rich Countries

Legacies of the Past

During the heyday of the energy boom, the energy rich developed highly segmented labor markets. Educated nationals were guaranteed jobs in the public sector. In the richest states, less-educated workers were also given government jobs; in the poorer states, such as Algeria and Iraq, the less educated worked in agriculture and the private sector. Foreign workers were imported to perform jobs that nationals were unable or unwilling to pursue. By the mid-1970s, foreign workers had already become a major part of the labor force.

The initial reliance on foreign labor emerged naturally in the Gulf states and Libya. During the oil boom, governments spent surging revenues on the construction of infrastructure, factories, and transfers to the population. These expenditures fueled demand for labor in construction, transport, wholesale and retail trade, personal services (maids, cooks, and drivers), and government services, such as education and health care. Employers turned to foreign workers to satisfy this burgeoning demand for labor. In the less populous states, employers were unable to find enough people with the skills needed to staff these jobs. Foreign workers, many from other Arab countries, with training in medicine, engineering, and administration were hired to satisfy the increased demand for skilled labor that accompanied the oil boom. The energy rich hired Palestinians and Egyptians to educate their children, provide medical care, and run their bureaucracies. Demand for unskilled, as well as skilled, labor grew rapidly, especially in construction, trucking, stevedoring, and trade. Locals were often unwilling to work in these occupations, especially the more onerous. Contractors found that foreign laborers worked harder, were more reliable, were more amenable to working these jobs, and were substantially cheaper than local workers.

In Iraq, political decisions led to importation of foreign labor. Saddam Hussein's forces invaded Iran in 1980, precipitating a conflict that lasted until 1988. Hundreds of thousands of Iraqi men were drafted into the army to prosecute the war. Saddam, intent on continuing national investment programs, hired foreign workers to construct roads, power plants, and other infrastructure. By the mid-1980s, 750,000 foreign laborers, mostly from Egypt, worked in Iraq.[40]

Because the statistical systems were often in their infancy at the time, it is difficult to find reliable time-series data on employment. However, a number of indicators show that the increase in demand for labor, local and foreign, during this period was staggering. The number of Arab migrant workers employed by the energy rich tripled between 1975, from 1.24 million in 1975 to 3.73 million in 1985, just before the bust.[41] During this period, Saudi Arabia employed two-thirds of the entire male labor force of Yemen, primarily in construction.[42]

The reliance on foreign labor was not precipitated by demand alone. Many locals were reluctant to take "dirty" jobs, preferring to seek work in the public sector. This preference for government jobs was encouraged by government policies. Most governments of the energy rich transferred some of their oil windfall to citizens by guaranteeing them jobs in the public sector. As late as the early 1990s, more than half the jobs for nationals in Algeria, Bahrain, and Saudi Arabia were in the public sector. The figures for Kuwait, Libya, and the other Persian Gulf states were even higher, running close to 90 percent in the case of Kuwait.[43] Because citizens were given government allowances for children and provided free housing, electricity, and subsidized health care, the imperative to work was missing in the wealthier countries. Consequently, interest in private-sector employment, especially if it entailed unpleasant working conditions or substantial effort, was limited.

The more-difficult economic times of the 1980s and 1990s in the energy-rich countries resulted in an exodus of foreign workers and declines in real public-sector wages. In Saudi Arabia, the extent of the decline in employment during the oil bust is striking. Total employment fell from 3.93 million in 1987, the first year for which data are available, to only 2.50 million in 1995, a fall of more than one-third.[44] By the late 1980s, Iraq no longer hired foreign labor; by the 1990s, impoverished Iraqis were seeking work outside of Iraq in the Persian Gulf or in OECD countries. Libya expelled Egyptians and other foreign nationals in 1995, ostensibly for political reasons, but also to open up employment opportunities for locals. In the smaller Persian Gulf states, although the numbers of foreign workers were down from the 1970s and 1980s, foreign workers still comprised most of the labor force. However, some skilled expatriates were replaced by locals.

Many governments could no longer afford to provide jobs to all citizens. In Algeria, the government had to cut the share of public-sector wages in total wages from three-fourths to

---

[40] Richards and Waterbury, 1996, p. 370.

[41] Richards and Waterbury, 1996, pp. 372–375.

[42] Chaudhry, 1997, p. 196.

[43] Richards and Waterbury, 1996, p. 139.

[44] IMF, "Saudi Arabia," *International Financial Statistics*, undated.

one-half as the government faced budgetary constraints. Young Algerians sought work abroad because of poor prospects at home. By 2001, half a million Algerian nationals were legally living in France; many more were there illegally.[45]

Problems of the Present

Figure 3.13 shows unemployment rates for a number of the energy-rich countries. As can be seen, changes in labor policies have resulted in sharp declines in unemployment rates in Algeria. The Persian Gulf states have had lower rates of unemployment than the more populous of the energy rich because so much of their labor is imported. Expatriate labor is tightly controlled: In most instances, the government provides a work permit only for a particular job in a specific company for a limited period, often three years. Once the contract ends, the worker must return to his or her home country and is permitted to return only if given a new work permit. Thus, expatriate workers are fully employed. In contrast, nationals, especially recent high school graduates or married women in their mid-20s, often report high unemployment rates, as they find it difficult to find a job that meets their expectations or desired conditions for work.

All the energy rich are experiencing large inflows of new entrants into their labor forces, as discussed in Chapter Two. These young people often take considerable time to find jobs. Among the energy rich, the numbers of nationals of working age rose by 3.3 percent per year between 1990 and 2006. Between 2006 and 2020, the population of working age will continue to rise by a projected 2.4 percent per year.

Figure 3.13
Unemployment Rates in the Energy Rich

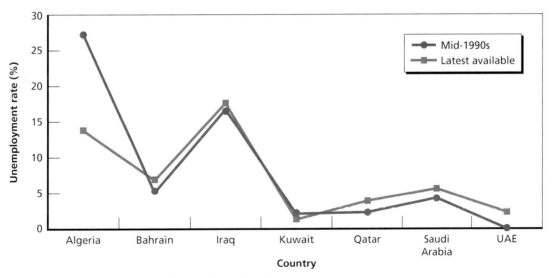

SOURCES: International Labour Office and World Bank data.
NOTE: Data listed are 2007 for Algeria and Saudi Arabia; 2006 for Bahrain, Iraq, and Kuwait; 2004 for Qatar; and 2000 for the UAE.
RAND TR912-3.13

---

[45] Organisation for Economic Co-Operation and Development (OECD), *Trends in International Migration: Continuous Reporting System on Migration*, Paris, 2001.

Despite the challenge posed by the large number of new labor market entrants, high rates of unemployment in Algeria and Libya have been driven by structural problems, not just the influx of new entrants. Much of the problem of slow job creation on the part of the private sector can be traced to the legal system and the public sector. Governments in the region have imposed minimum wages and strictures on firing and hiring that have discouraged businesses from hiring and entrepreneurs from investing. The entire region, energy rich and energy poor alike, has failed to develop much in the way of large, private companies or to attract much in the way of foreign direct investment.[46] The reason is the same: Private-sector companies have to battle with high barriers to trade, high costs for financial transactions, and a myriad of government regulations on normal business operations. As a consequence, employment by large private-sector firms tends to constitute a small share of total employment. Consequently, new job market entrants have much more-limited opportunities than young people in regions with more-congenial business climates: Graduates can wait for a public-sector job to open up while relying on their families for their livelihood, scratch out a living in the informal economy, or go abroad for work, but they have little prospect of finding a salaried position in a large private firm because so few of these companies operate in the region.

Public-sector employment has had a number of detrimental effects on private-sector employment. Overstaffing in the public sector is a major reason for declining factor productivity. More people are hired to complete the same amount of work. To pay the salaries of these people, the state diverts resources from potentially more-productive uses, such as investing or purchasing goods or services produced by the private sector. As noted earlier, overstaffing has made it easier for civil servants to spend time devising regulations designed to extort bribes from businesses. Public-sector pay scales have often exceeded the value of output provided by the employee. Consequently, private-sector businesses find the labor market for skilled local labor overpriced. They respond by importing labor or failing to develop potentially profitable lines of business. In some instances, government wages act as a legal benchmark for equivalent private-sector wages, pushing up wage costs to potentially unprofitable levels.

Public-sector employment in the energy rich has contributed to a mismatch between how many of their nationals wish to work and what employers need in terms of labor discipline and effort. In many of the energy rich, nationals are still reluctant to take jobs involving manual labor. Young men with high school or college educations prefer to seek openings in government employment rather than take lower-status jobs in the private sector. Although levels of education have improved, in some instances, work discipline and effort have not. Governments have the wherewithal to prevent citizens being abandoned to their own devices but have failed to generate sustained increases in economic growth that would generate steadier, more-remunerative sources of employment and increases in incomes.

The large role of energy in these economies does not necessarily have a detrimental effect on employment. It is true that efficiently run energy sectors are often not large employers. The extraction of oil and natural gas is a capital-intensive process. Once a well has been drilled, collection systems and pipelines constructed, and export terminals set up, efficiently run operations employ few people. However, in many countries, key economic sectors are capital intensive. In Canada, two key exports—wheat and natural gas—utilize little in the way of labor.

---

[46] According to the United Nations Development Programme, *Arab Human Development Report 2002*, New York: United Nations Development Programme, Regional Bureau for Arab States, 2002, p. 87, the Arab world is home to less than 1 percent of global foreign direct investment.

Computer chips, corn, and chemicals from the United States, iron ore from Brazil, and coal from Australia are all capital-intensive sectors. In these economies, other, more–labor-intensive sectors, such as retailing, business services, and health care, generate job growth. The problem for the energy rich is not energy wealth but that government employment and policies have discouraged the private sector from hiring or, if it hires, filled jobs with foreign workers.

CHAPTER FOUR

The Energy Poor: Prospects for Economic Growth

We classify the remaining countries in this study of the Arab world as the energy poor: Egypt, Jordan, Lebanon, Morocco, Syria, Tunisia, the entities of the West Bank and Gaza, and Yemen. Although some of these countries export energy, exports of other goods, worker remittances, and incomes from services play much more-important roles in their external accounts than they do among the energy-rich states. Because these energy-poor countries have not had the luxury of oil revenues to pay for government expenditures and transfers to the population, their governments have faced more-difficult trade-offs in economic policies than the energy-rich countries have. They have responded in different ways, with some having begun to liberalize their economies and others having continued to pursue the statist policies of the past.

In this chapter, we evaluate the performance of the energy-poor economies, contrasting economic performance among those countries that have liberalized more aggressively and those where the state has continued to intervene heavily in the economy. We then examine differences in economic policies across the countries with an eye to identifying best practices. We end by looking at labor-force issues and prospects.

When we examine the energy-poor countries in our report, we find the following:

- Per capita GDPs are lower in the energy poor than among the energy rich, but, since 1990, the economic performance of the energy poor has been superior to that of the energy rich.
- One of the keys to rapid economic growth is openness to foreign trade. Energy-poor nations with more-open trade policies have performed better than those that have impeded cross-border flows of goods, ideas, technologies, and corporate practices.
- The energy poor have generally had greater difficulty maintaining macroeconomic stability; many have suffered balance-of-payments crises followed by sharp devaluations and high rates of inflation.
- The energy poor have perpetuated most of the microeconomic policy mistakes of the energy rich, but, lacking substantial revenues from oil, the economic consequences of not rectifying their policy mistakes have been more severe.
- However, *some* of the energy poor have taken a more-aggressive approach to making policy changes to improve the environment for economic growth, having begun to remove price controls and subsidies, reduce barriers to entry for private businesses, liberalize trade, and privatize state-owned enterprises, albeit not always with the greatest enthusiasm.
- In contrast to the energy rich, not all the energy poor have enjoyed substantially more-rapid economic growth between 2000 and 2008 than between 1990 and 2000, but, in

either of the future scenarios used, if growth continues at the rates of the recent past, the energy poor will enjoy appreciable increases in per capita incomes.

- Institutional reform will be an important factor determining future economic growth, but, for most of the energy poor, security, internal and external, will remain a key determinant of growth.
- During the 1990s, rapid growth in the labor force took place at a time of modest increases in output, causing real wages to fall or stagnate in many countries; now, increased demand for expatriate Arab labor from the energy rich, coupled with better domestic economic performance from the energy poor, has created a better environment for employment and wage growth,
- The extent to which economic activity and incomes increase will have a crucial effect on the direction and extent of pressure for political change.

We discuss these findings in more detail in the remainder of this chapter.

Economic Performance of the Energy-Poor Countries

Economic Output of the Energy-Poor Countries

Egypt, the largest and most-populous country in the region, also has the largest economy, accounting for 38 percent of aggregate GDP among the energy poor (Figure 4.1). Morocco, which ranks second to Egypt in terms of both population and land mass, accounts for more than 22 percent of output among this group. The economies of Jordan, the Palestinian territories, and Yemen—with GDPs of less than $20 billion—are smaller than the value of output from a typical U.S. city of 500,000 inhabitants.

Figure 4.1
GDPs of the Energy-Poor Countries in 2007

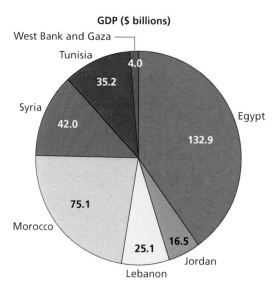

SOURCE: Calculated from IMF data.
NOTE: Data for Yemen are for 2005.
RAND *TR912-4.1*

Per capita GDP, even using PPP exchange rates, ranges more widely among these countries than it does among the energy rich. Lebanon and Tunisia are upper-middle-income developing countries. In contrast, since the second intifada, economic conditions in the Palestinian territories have regressed to such a degree that the West Bank and Gaza are best classified as low-income developing entities, as is Yemen. Egypt, Jordan, Morocco, and Syria are classified as lower-middle-income developing countries.

Per capita GDP in the energy-poor countries remains substantially below their better-endowed neighbors at both market and PPP exchange rates (Figure 4.2), although most of the energy poor are wealthier than Iraq. Putting aside the case of Iraq, the only exceptions are Lebanon, which has a higher per capita GDP at market exchange rates than Algeria, and Tunisia, which has a higher per capita GDP than Algeria at PPP exchange rates. Oil wealth adds appreciably to per capita incomes in the energy-rich countries.

Economic Growth of the Energy-Poor Countries

Although, by and large, per capita GDPs remains lower in the energy poor than in the energy-rich countries, between 1989 and 1999, per capita GDP rose more rapidly among the former than the latter. Between 1999 and 2007, growth in the energy poor kept pace with the energy rich, even as the latter enjoyed more-rapid growth. Average growth in per capita GDP weighted by 2005 dollar GDP ran 1.9 percent per year in the energy-poor countries between 1989 and 1999 (Figure 4.3). In the energy-rich countries, per capita GDP rose at roughly half that rate, 1.0 percent per annum (as shown earlier in the counterpart graphic for the energy-rich countries in Figure 3.8 in Chapter Three). Between 1999 and 2007, rates were 3.0 and 2.9 percent, respectively. The energy poor have registered more-uniform growth. Since 1999, all the countries except the West Bank and Gaza have enjoyed increases in per capita GDP of 2 percent or more.

Figure 4.2
Per Capita GDP in the Energy Poor

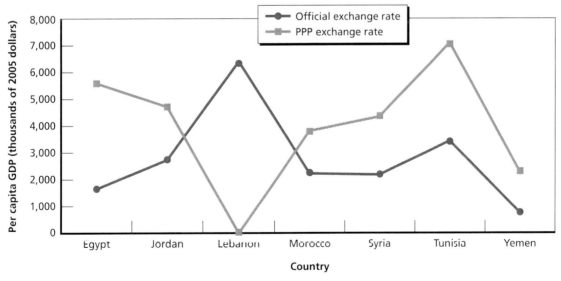

SOURCE: Calculated from IMF data.
NOTE: Data for Yemen are for 2005.
RAND TR912-4.2

Figure 4.3
Average Annual Changes in Per Capita GDP in Energy-Poor Countries

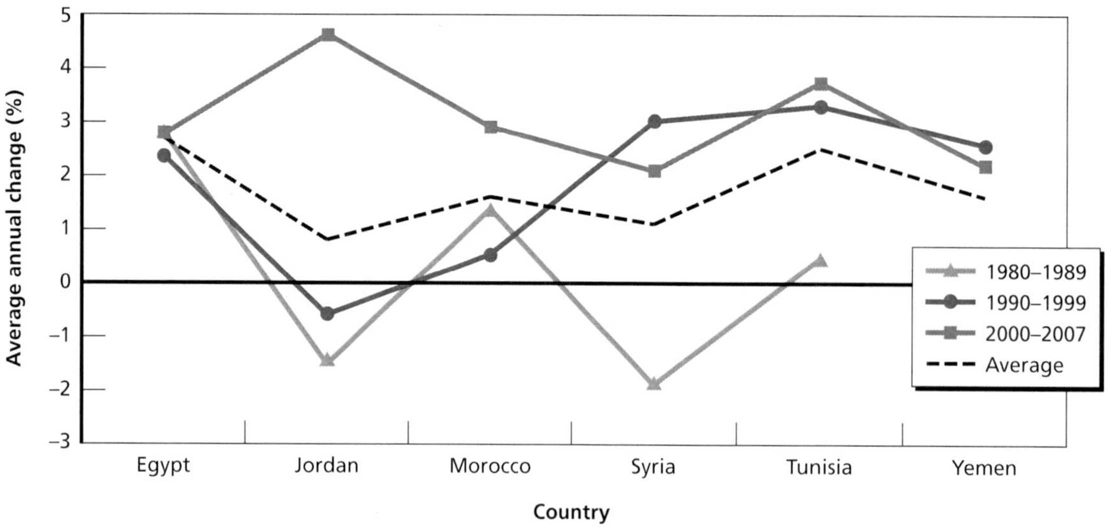

SOURCE: Calculated from IMF data.
NOTE: Data for Egypt start in 1982; data for Yemen start in 1990 and end in 2005.
RAND *TR912-4.3*

Despite superior economic performance by the energy poor since 1990, growth patterns in the energy poor and energy rich have exhibited similar trends over the past half-century, primarily because of the economic linkages between the two groups of countries, although economic swings for the energy rich have been more exaggerated. In both groups of countries, economic growth was strong in the 1950s and 1960s as the Arab states benefited from improvements in educational attainments, investment in infrastructure, and rising exports. During the course of the oil boom of the 1970s, growth became symbiotic: Although interregional trade within the Arab world is far lower than in other regions,[1] other economic ties have been strong. The energy-poor Arab states became very large exporters of labor to the energy rich during the oil boom. The "frontline" states, those bordering Israel, also benefited from the largesse of the energy rich as the latter provided substantial grants and loans to support the armies and governments of those neighbors of Israel that opposed peace.[2]

Rates of growth in per capita GDP fell sharply in the 1980s; in some countries, they continued to decline in the 1990s. Hard times in the oil-exporting countries sharply reduced demand for labor from the energy poor. International events also played a role. Egyptians, who had been recruited to work in Iraq during the Iraq-Iran War as Iraqi men were conscripted by the armed forces, went home by the end of the 1980s because Iraq could no longer afford their services. The Kuwaitis expelled Palestinians after the 1990–1991 Gulf War due to the perception of a security risk given Saddam Hussein's linking of the war to the Palestinian cause. Yemenis found it increasingly difficult to find work in Saudi Arabia and the Gulf states given their government's neutrality in the 1990–1991 Gulf War, a decision that was interpreted by

---

[1] Rodolphe Blavy, *Trade in the Mashreq: An Empirical Examination*, Washington, D.C.: International Monetary Fund, Middle Eastern Department, working paper 01/163, October 1, 2001, p. 3.

[2] The biggest benefactor, Egypt, lost this support when its government signed the Camp David accords. Assistance from the United States helped to fill this gap.

the Gulf monarchies as supporting Saddam's invasion. Syria suffered from sharp reductions in aid from the Gulf states following the collapse in world market oil prices in the early 1980s and Syria's "defection" to Iran during the Iran-Iraq War.

The Role of International Trade and Financial Flows

One of the keys to rapid economic growth is openness to foreign trade. All nations, but especially those with smaller economies, benefit from gains from trade and cross-border flows of ideas, technologies, and corporate practices. By opening up opportunities for trade, in aggregate, consumer welfare rises and businesses' opportunities for increasing sales and output are enhanced. Because of the small size of the economies of the energy poor, future economic growth in these countries will depend on their ability to sell goods and services abroad.

Earnings from exports of goods and services, incomes from labor and capital, and transfers run from 43 to 101 percent of the GDPs of the energy-poor states (Figure 4.4). These percentages are not particularly high: The average percentage of a developing country's GDP made up by exports of goods and services is about 70 percent.[3] In fact, the ratios for countries other than Jordan and Lebanon are on the low side. In contrast to most other countries of the world, exports of goods from this group of countries are often less important than exports of services. When only exports of goods are considered, export-to-GDP ratios are low, running from just 16 percent of GDP in the case of Lebanon to 43 percent in the case of Tunisia. Tunisia's ratio reflects the success of its export zones in increasing exports to the European Union (EU).

The patterns of exports from these countries are fairly uniform. Similar to the energy-rich countries, exports tend to be concentrated in a few products: labor-intensive, relatively unsophisticated manufactured goods, such as clothing and shoes, or agricultural and mineral commodities, such as cotton from Egypt or phosphates from Morocco.

Figure 4.4
Exports of Goods, Services, and Transfers as a Share of GDP in 2007

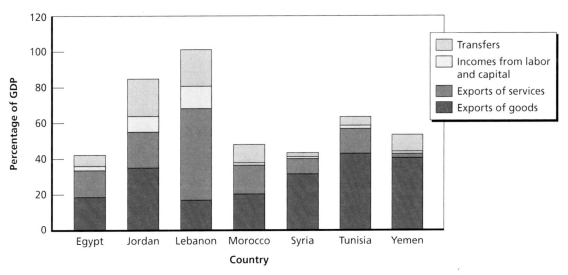

SOURCE: Calculated from IMF data.
NOTE: Data for Yemen are for 2005; for Syria, 2006.
RAND *TR912-4.4*

---

[3] Blavy, 2001, p. 4.

The trade performance of the energy poor as measured by shares of global trade has been similar to that of Latin America but inferior to Asia's. The energy poor's share of world exports was 0.88 percent in 1970 and 0.85 percent in 2006. There was little variation around this number in the intervening years. In contrast, Asia's share of global exports rose from 5.7 percent to 23.0 percent over this same period.[4]

Service incomes loom large in the balances of payments of these countries partly because of geography and history and in part because of poor export performance. Tourism is an important industry for all the energy-poor states except Syria and Yemen. Its important role has social as well as economic implications. On the one hand, it provides large numbers of jobs for individuals with a broad range of skills, from hotel managers to translators to camel drivers. Tourism generates 6 percent of Tunisia's GDP and employs 13.5 percent of the labor force, directly or indirectly.[5] On the other hand, the contrast between how foreign tourists behave on beach vacations and Islamic social mores can be stark. Tourist sites have often been targets for terrorists. Consequently, a number of these states, including Egypt, Morocco, and Tunisia, are economically vulnerable to incidents of terrorism, as demonstrated by the sharp declines in tourism following the 1997 attacks in Luxor and the 2003 attacks in Casablanca.

Sales of transport services—most notably, transit fees from tolls for the use of the Suez Canal in the case of Egypt and pipeline transit charges in the case of Syria—are also important sources of foreign earnings. In Egypt, tolls from the Suez Canal provided 10 percent of government income as late as 2003.[6] However, these tolls have not succeeded in making Egypt a "rentier" state. Although these revenues ease fiscal pressures on the Egyptian government, they have not eliminated the need for the Egyptian government to levy other taxes. In fact, as the Egyptian economy has grown, tolls have become increasingly less important for financing the government budget.

Remittances from emigrant labor to the rest of the world play a major role in the local economies (Figure 4.5). In Jordan, Lebanon, and Morocco, remittances provide as much as one-third of total earnings of foreign exchange. The Gulf oil states are major sources of these funds. More than $20 billion is remitted from the Arab world annually; Saudi Arabia accounts for nearly three-fourths of this total. Saudi Arabia is now the second-largest source of remittances of any country in the world, following the United States.[7]

The important role played by remittances reflects the symbiotic relationship between the energy rich and the energy poor. Egyptians and the Palestinian community, as well as the Yemenis, have supplied many of the workers, skilled and unskilled, that the energy rich have employed to build and staff their modernizing economies, especially in the 1970s and early 1980s. By the end of the 1980s, more than one-third of the labor force in Egypt had worked abroad.[8] Morocco and Algeria, an energy-rich country, have also benefited from substantial earnings from remittances, although, in the case of these two countries, migrants head for

---

[4] IMF, *International Financial Statistics*, various years.

[5] IMF, *Tunisia: 2003 Article IV Consultation—Staff Report, Staff Supplement, Public Information Notice on the Executive Board Discussion and Statement by the Executive Director for Tunisia*, country report 03/259, 2003a, p. 10.

[6] IMF, "Egypt," *International Financial Statistics*, Washington, D.C.: April 2004a, p. 372.

[7] Dilip Ratha, "Workers' Remittances: An Important and Stable Source of External Development Finance," *Global Development Finance 2003*, World Bank, 2003, pp. 157–176. This squares with IMF reporting as well.

[8] Richards and Waterbury, 1996, p. 370.

Figure 4.5
Official Remittances for Selected Arab Countries, 2005

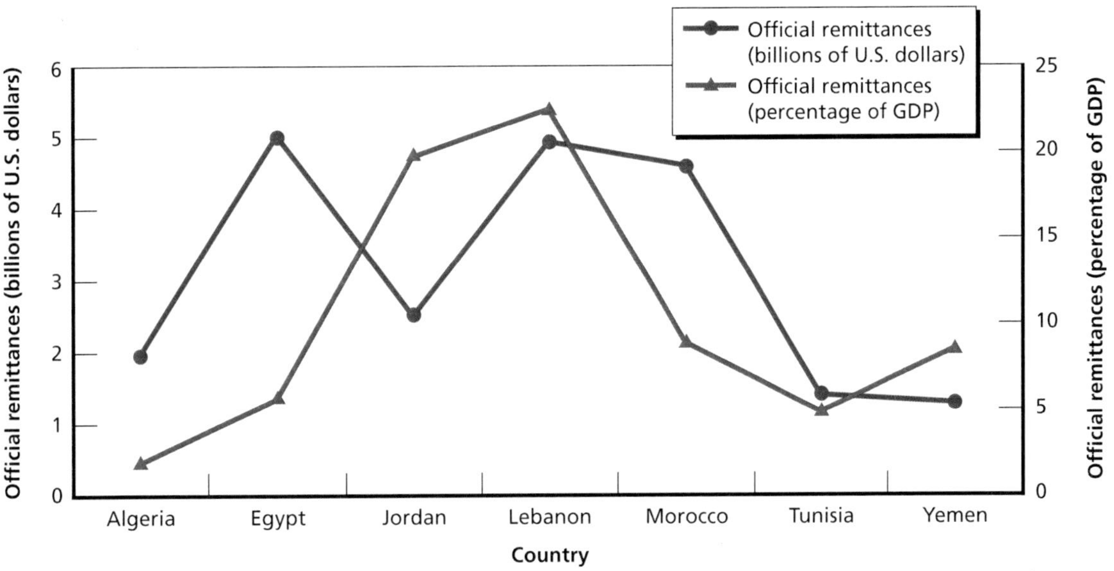

SOURCE: World Bank, 2007.
RAND TR912-4.5

Europe rather than the Persian Gulf states. In all these countries, domestic economic growth depends heavily on foreign demand for labor and the ensuing inflows of remittances. While the energy poor have benefited from periods of boom in the energy rich, they suffer during periods of bust. When the price of oil has fallen precipitously, as occurred in the mid-1990s, or the Persian Gulf has been consumed in conflict in which regional states are forced to take sides, labor-exporting countries are hit hard.

Foreign assistance—both from other countries in the region and from donors farther afield, such as the United States, the European Union, and the former Soviet Union—has also contributed significantly to the economies of many of these countries. In the early 1970s, Jordan's government received almost as much money from donors as it collected from its own tax revenues. During that period, foreign grants to Jordan's budget ran 6 to 8 percent of GDP. Morocco has also been a large recipient of foreign assistance.

Why Did the Energy-Poor Economies Perform as They Did Between 1980 and 2000?

As noted in the previous chapter, security, sound macroeconomic policies, and an efficient institutional and regulatory environment are important determinants of economic growth. Similar to the energy rich, the economic performance of the energy poor has frequently suffered from lack of security and a poor business environment. However, in contrast to the energy rich, these countries have generally had greater difficulty in maintaining macroeconomic stability.

Security. The economies of the Palestinian territories and Lebanon tend to fluctuate with levels of violence. Although the second intifada's effects on Israel have been grim, the consequences for the West Bank and Gaza have been horrific. From the time the second intifada began in September 2000 through 2002, gross national income, which includes earnings from Palestinian labor in Israel and elsewhere, fell 28 percent. Combined with the increase in population, per capita income in 2002 was less than two-thirds of its September 2000 level.[9] In particular, the intifadas and repeated Israeli interventions have hit the tourism sector—a key sector for the West Bank—hard.

Lebanon's economy also bears the scars of conflict. Reliable economic data for periods of conflict are limited, but what data are available are depressing. Lebanon's exports in 1974 were $1.636 billion. After the civil war broke out in 1975, exports fell by two-thirds to just $546 million in 1976. As of 2002, they had still failed to return to their 1974 level in nominal dollars; in real terms, exports in 2002 were still less than one-third their pre–civil war level. Roughly 10 percent of Lebanon's pre–civil war population emigrated in the 15 years following the beginning of the civil war.[10]

Yemen's tumultuous history has been a major reason for its poverty. Even at PPP exchange rates, its per capita GDP of only $2,276 in 2005 dollars is less than half of Egypt's and two-thirds of Morocco's, the two other poorest energy-poor states. Yemen, which was unified in just 1990, has suffered a series of civil wars, the latest of which erupted in 1994.[11] Although data on GDP before 1990 are not available, the constant fighting and unstable political situation have kept incomes low and triggered capital flight, as many Yemenis prefer to keep abroad what little wealth they have.

Small states situated next to states in turmoil frequently suffer collateral economic damage. Jordan is a case in point. Despite one of the better track records in terms of economic policies, macro and micro, the per capita GDP of Jordan in 2005 was 10.4 percent less than it had been 23 years earlier. Jordan was hammered by the effects on its exports from the international trade embargo on Iraq following Iraq's invasion of Kuwait. It also absorbed a flood of Palestinians expelled from the Persian Gulf states after the Gulf War. These individuals, who had previously provided very substantial inflows of remittances, were suddenly unemployed. Statistics on transfers, which include remittances, tell the story: Transfers from abroad fell from more than $2 billion annually at the height of the oil boom to $1.5 billion at the end of the 1980s, to below $1 billion in 1991, the year of the Gulf War. More recently, Jordan and Syria have become havens for refugees fleeing from Iraq. It is difficult to estimate the impact that refugee flows have on Jordan's economy beyond stating that they have strained Jordan's labor market, public services, and the housing market in Amman.[12]

Monetary and Fiscal Policies. With some notable exceptions on both sides, the energy-poor countries have struggled more than the energy rich to maintain sound macroeconomic policies. For the energy rich, export earnings from oil and gas provide a solid revenue and export base that have made it easier for these countries to keep their fiscal balances and, hence, inflation under control. Energy exports have also provided the energy rich with better access to international capital markets in difficult economic times, making it possible for them to obtain bridge financing during periods of fiscal stress. The energy poor have had less wiggle room. When fiscal and external imbalances have gotten out of hand, most of the energy poor

[9] World Bank, *The Palestinian Economy and the Prospects for Its Recovery: Economic Monitoring Report to the Ad Hoc Liaison Committee*, No. 1, December 2005, p. 7.

[10] U.S. Census Bureau, 2008.

[11] Chaudhry, 1997, pp. 301–304.

[12] Patricia Weiss Fagen, *Iraqi Refugees: Seeking Stability in Syria and Jordan*, Doha: Institute for the Study of International Migration, Center for International and Regional Studies, 2007, pp. 12–14.

have suffered balance-of-payments crises, which have been followed by sharp devaluations and high rates of inflation.

In the 1970s, there was not much difference in inflation rates between the energy rich and the energy poor. But between 1980 and 1990, inflation rates in the energy poor soared (Figure 4.6), while they remained under control in the energy rich. The inflation of the 1980s was precipitated by current-account and budgetary imbalances. For example, inflation in Egypt peaked at 24.1 percent in 1986 after a string of budget deficits in the range of 10 percent of GDP and current-account deficits of 4 percent or more of GDP. Inflation hit 60 percent in Syria in 1987, following a similar pattern of large budget and current-account deficits (Figure 4.7).

These countries chose to print money to cover budget deficits (and suffer the ensuing consequences for inflation) because they lacked the capacity to raise tax revenues and the will to cut government expenditures. During their peak inflation years, government expenditures and revenues constituted much more-sizable shares of GDP in Egypt and Syria than they did in Jordan, Morocco, and Tunisia, countries that followed sounder macroeconomic policies in the 1980s (Figure 4.7). Whereas government expenditures were well over 40 percent of GDP in Egypt and Syria, in the other countries, they ran one-third of GDP or less. Improved performance on inflation in the first three countries is due in great part to more-austere fiscal policies: By 2006, expenditures as a share of GDP had fallen below 40 percent of GDP in all the energy-poor countries.

Microeconomic Policies: What Have the Energy Poor Done Wrong? The energy poor have perpetuated most of the economic policy mistakes of the energy rich. Many of these policy mistakes have nothing to do with energy. However, lacking substantial revenues from oil, the economic consequences for the energy poor of not rectifying their policy mistakes have been more severe.

Figure 4.6
Average Inflation Rates in the Energy Poor

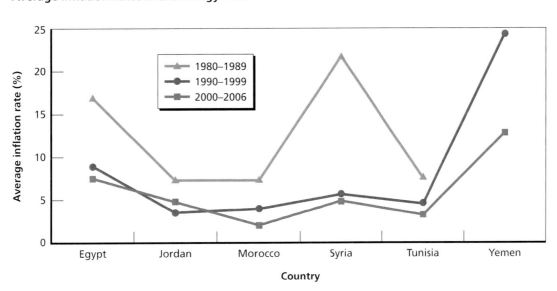

SOURCE: Calculated from IMF data.
NOTE: Data for Yemen and Syria are through 2007.
RAND *TR912-4.6*

Figure 4.7
Government Expenditures as a Share of GDP

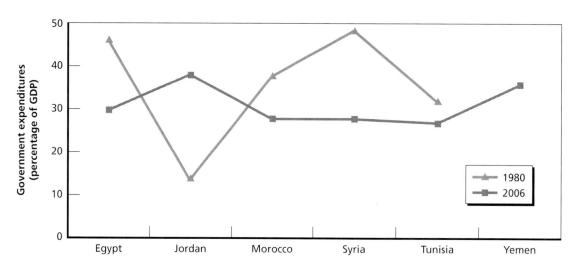

SOURCE: Calculated from IMF data.
NOTE: Data for Yemen and Syria are through 2007.
RAND TR912-4.7

Price Controls and Subsidies. Like the energy rich, the energy poor have employed price subsidies and price controls to placate domestic political groups and to provide a comprehensive, if expensive, social safety net—one they can ill afford. The largest subsidies and price distortions exist for food, agricultural products, and energy. Although food-subsidy programs have reduced malnutrition, they do so at great cost. In the region as a whole, food price subsidies account for between 1 and 5 percent of GDP, equivalent to as much as one-fifth of total government expenditures.[13] The programs are poorly targeted: On average, 60 to 80 percent of the expenditures on food subsidies in this region have gone to upper-income groups.[14] In light of the other fiscal needs of these countries, this is a poor allocation of resources.

Price distortions generated by these programs have substantial opportunity, as well as fiscal, costs. Although not as egregious as the Saudi Arabian programs that subsidized wheat growers, price controls on food and agricultural products have had detrimental effects on the energy poor just as they have had for the energy rich. In Morocco and Tunisia, farmers of sugar beets and wheat have been protected from foreign competition by very high tariffs, 84 to 157 percent in the case of Morocco, while sugar and flour are sold below cost. The government picks up the difference.[15] Because of smuggling and other forms of leakage, sometimes the government pays smugglers the higher domestic price for smuggled wheat from abroad, with resulting negative consequences for the budget. The subsidies and price controls also have negative consequences for agricultural efficiency and, in some cases, incomes. Farmers grow too much of the subsidized crops or too little of the crop subject to price controls. As a consequence, agricultural sectors often stagnate, failing to respond to market signals either

---

[13] World Bank, *Consumer Food Subsidy Programs in the MENA Region*, Washington, D.C., report 19561-MNA, November 12, 1999, p. 10.

[14] World Bank, 1999, p. ii.

[15] World Bank, 1999, p. 11.

from domestic consumers or from the world market. This is especially troubling because rural inhabitants tend to be poorer than urban dwellers. These policies serve to widen the gap, contributing to economic dissatisfaction and migration to urban areas.

A number of the energy poor provide subsidies on refined oil products, especially diesel fuel and household heating oil. These have been substantial in the cases of Egypt, Jordan, and Syria, often running a few percentage points of GDP.[16] These subsidies encourage the consumption of the subsidized products, which, in the case of Jordan and, more recently, Egypt, have to be imported. In some instances, prices were set so low that wholesalers collaborate in smuggling expensively imported diesel fuel sold at domestically subsidized prices to such countries as Turkey, where prices are much higher. However, governments have begun to reduce these costs. The Egyptian government raised fuel prices by 25 to 90 percent in 2006, in the face of substantial popular opposition.[17] The Moroccan government has relinked domestic fuel prices to the world market price of oil, limiting its financial exposure to providing fuel subsidies.[18]

Unlike in the United States, where widespread car ownership means that reductions in gasoline prices benefit lower-income segments, in such countries as Egypt, where car ownership remains concentrated among the more wealthy, gasoline subsidies are captured by the better off. The upper 2 percent of Egyptian households by income receive an average of 1,800 Egyptian pounds per household (approximately $320) annually from that country's fuel subsidies, the figure drops to just 234 Egyptian pounds (approximately $42) per household for the lower-income groups.[19]

Barriers to Entry. The energy poor do not have a stellar track record when it comes to stimulating private-sector activity. Because the governments have often used government employment as the first resort for jobs for new entrants to the labor market, state administrations are bloated. With little real work to do, civil servants have been noted for using their positions to impede registration procedures, schedule unwarranted inspections, or initiate tax audits. To survive these inspections, private businesses pay bribes. Because the judicial system is often corrupt and inefficient, private businesses lack effective recourse in the courts; cases can stretch out for decades. The resistance to change in these bureaucracies is stunning. Reportedly, one Egyptian minister requested that most of his staff stay home (with pay) because they were doing nothing productive at work. Faced with the prospect of losing income from bribes, his staff revolted. The minister was summarily fired.

To enforce price controls and provide subsidies, the governments have had to set up large regulatory apparatuses in an effort to prevent "leakage" of subsidies to unintended parties. The controls on trade, especially imports, that ensue impose large transaction costs on private

---

[16] Karim A. Nashashibi, *Fiscal Revenues in South Mediterranean Arab Countries: Vulnerabilities and Growth Potential*, Washington, D.C.: International Monetary Fund, working paper 02/67, April 2002, p. 15.

[17] IMF, *Arab Republic of Egypt: 2007 Article IV Consultation—Staff Report, Staff Statement, Public Information Notice on the Executive Board Discussion, and Statement by the Executive Director for the Arab Republic of Egypt*, Washington, D.C., country report 07/380, December 2007b, p. 11.

[18] IMF, *Morocco: 2007 Article IV Consultation—Staff Report, Staff Statement, Public Information Notice on the Executive Board Discussion, and Statement by the Executive Director for Morocco*, Washington, D.C., country report 07/323, September 2007a, p. 9.

[19] Sherine Abdel-Razek, "The Cost of Budgeting," *al-Ahram Weekly*, June 19, 2008.

industry—in some cases, closing off private-sector activities. For example, the grain trade is so heavily regulated in many of the energy poor that entry or exit by private-sector firms is rare.

As in the energy rich, government contracting tends to favor firms with connections, precluding competition and entry of new businesses. Syria and Egypt, in particular, have made it difficult for new companies to enter markets, especially those involving government licenses or procurement because traditional providers are so firmly embedded.

Although some countries experience less corruption than others, with the partial exception of Jordan and Tunisia, the energy poor have not been easy countries in which to do business, as shown by their rankings by Transparency International (Figure 4.8). The smaller Persian Gulf oil exporters score much better than most of the energy poor.

Taxation has been another factor retarding the growth of the private sector. Because these governments do not have ready access to substantial revenues from oil exports, taxation of private-sector activities is crucial for budget revenues. These taxes are often designed to be complicated because tax inspectors manipulate the system to seek bribes.

Onerous labor laws have also retarded the growth of the private sector. Private firms are reluctant to hire in good times if they face legal barriers to downsizing their workforce during bad. In many countries, firms respond to strictures on firing by subcontracting or seeking extralegal ways of avoiding formal employment contracts. In other instances, they choose to hire fewer employees than they otherwise would.[20]

Barriers to Trade. The relatively low level of exports as a share of GDP and as a share of external earnings in most of these countries is a consequence of counterproductive trade policies. Since the 1960s, most countries in the region have heavily protected their domestic mar-

Figure 4.8
Corruption Rankings

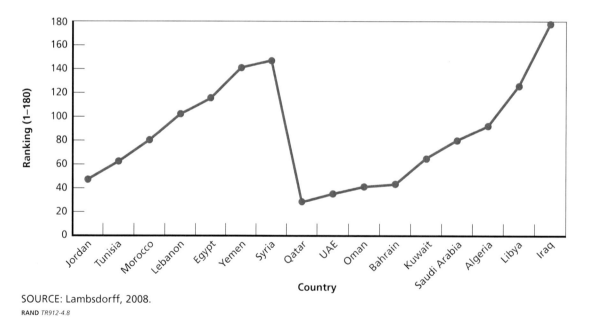

SOURCE: Lambsdorff, 2008.

RAND *TR912-4.8*

---

[20] P.-R. Agénor, M. K. Nabli, T. Yousef, and H. T. Jensen, *Labor Market Reforms, Growth, and Unemployment in Labor-Exporting Countries in the Middle East and North Africa*, World Bank: Policy Research Working Paper 3328, June 2004, p. 18.

kets. By protecting their domestic markets, countries impede the growth of exports. Exporters find it difficult to import the components and materials they need to make their products competitive. Tariffs, quotas, and administrative barriers make the domestic market more attractive and discourage foreign and domestic companies from investing in export industries; export growth suffers. Egypt, which followed highly protectionist policies until the early 1990s, is an example of the consequences of these policies. Egypt's dollar exports grew just 1.8 percent between 1980 and 1990, a truly miserable performance.

These countries have employed a complicated array of barriers to protect domestic industries, to tax imports, or to provide favored importers with special access to local markets, including import licenses, import quotas, high tariffs, and multiple exchange rate regimes. Import permits and quotas are the most ham-handed way of controlling imports and one of the most prone to corruption. They allow the government to pick and choose which company will be able to benefit from selling into the protected local market by steering permits and quotas to the company of the government's choice.

Tariffs have been an appreciable source of government revenues among the energy poor, running more than half of government revenues in the case of Lebanon and one-fifth to one-third of revenues for most of the other countries.[21] In many instances, tariffs have been high and highly differentiated as governments have sought to both collect revenue and protect favored domestic markets.

High, differentiated tariffs have distorted signals to local entrepreneurs concerning what to produce. For example, very high tariffs on automobiles in Egypt encouraged the creation of "screwdriver" operations: small local assembly operations that import disassembled automobiles, screw the parts together, and sell the vehicle on the local market at double the wholesale cost of a new imported car before tariffs. These operations tend to destroy value because the cost of the kit might be higher than the cost of a fully assembled vehicle. Selecting a few, relatively low tariff rates for all commodities reduces the distortion to market signals caused by tariffs.

Many of the energy-poor countries have used multitier exchange rates to restrain the cost of politically sensitive imports. Syria has a long tradition in this regard. By setting an official rate that is lower than the market rate, be that set in officially sanctioned markets or on the street, governments distort price signals to exporters and importers, resulting in a misallocation of foreign exchange and a reduction in welfare. Multiple exchange rate regimes provide implicit subsidies to importers that are able to purchase imports more cheaply than if they had to pay the market rate for foreign exchange. Exporters face implicit taxes because they receive less money than they would at market exchange rates. Hence, exporters are discouraged from selling abroad while importers are not encouraged to look for lower-cost domestic substitutes. These exchange rate regimes also create avenues for graft as exporters and importers bribe government employees so as to receive permission to buy or sell foreign exchange at the more-favorable rate. One reason that these regimes endure is the bureaucracy's desire not to lose this source of graft.

State-Directed Investments and State-Owned Companies. Like the energy rich, the energy poor have squandered resources on state-directed investments and on loss-making state-owned companies. Although the specific industries and operating problems differ, the

---

[21] Nashashibi, 2002, p. 11.

stories across the region have been the same. State-owned banks or banks with state or political connections usually pose the greatest problem. These banks take depositors' money and lend it to private individuals with political connections or to state-owned enterprises. Too frequently, the projects are ill conceived, poorly planned, and then poorly run. Because the projects are unprofitable, the borrowers are unable to repay their loans. The banks, in turn, then lack the funds to repay depositors. To forestall a collapse of the country's financial system, the state then steps in, replacing bad corporate debts with government bonds and closing or recapitalizing the banks. The economy suffers from the misallocation of scarce capital and the budget from the costs of servicing the higher levels of government debt.

Problems with state-controlled banks in the region are pervasive, and the costs of bailing them out large. In 2002, in Tunisia, more than half of all nonperforming loans were held by state-owned banks, which had underprovisioned for these loans (i.e., the state had to cover some of the loan losses).[22] In Egypt, the state-owned banks are burdened by the bad debts of state-owned enterprises.

The problems of the state-owned banks can usually be laid at the feet of state-owned enterprises. State-owned enterprises have played major roles in all the economies in the region except Lebanon's. For example, in 2002, the Moroccan government owned 688 enterprises. They contributed 12 percent of GDP in 2002 but, in aggregate, lost money, increasing the burden on the budget. In Egypt, despite a vigorous privatization program that began in the early 1990s, roughly one-third of GDP was still generated by state-owned enterprises in 2000.[23] Much of Syria's GDP is generated by state-owned companies as well. In all these countries, loss-making state-owned companies were kept afloat by loans from state-owned banks. Initially, loans were made for investments in plants and machinery, operations that frequently have not been profitable. Once up and operating, the banks are then pressed to cover operating losses as well, adding to their portfolio of bad loans.

Microeconomic Policies: What Have They Put Right? Like their energy-rich cousins, the energy poor have had a history of adopting economic policies that have served to reduce productivity growth. They, too, suffered from declines or stagnation in growth in factor productivity in the 1980s and 1990s.[24] However, lacking the ability to fall back on oil revenues, some of the energy poor have taken a more-aggressive approach to making policy changes to improve the environment for economic growth. They have begun to remove price controls and subsidies, reduce barriers to entry for private businesses, liberalize trade, and privatize state-owned enterprises, albeit not always with the greatest enthusiasm. In this section, we review some of the policy changes that the energy poor have gotten right and discuss what still remains to be done.

Reducing Price Controls and Subsidies. Arab governments have approached reducing subsidies, especially those on food, with trepidation, and not without reason. Reducing food subsidies and increasing prices triggered food riots in Egypt in 1977, in Morocco in 1981, in Tunisia in 1983, in Algeria in 1988, and in Jordan in both 1989 and 1996. In Egypt, the

---

[22] IMF, 2003a, p. 19.

[23] World Bank, "Memorandum of the International Bank for Reconstruction and Development and the International Financial Corporation to the Executive Directors on a Country Strategy for the Arab Republic of Egypt," Report 22163-EGT, Washington, D.C.: World Bank, June 5, 2001, p. 24.

[24] Das Gupta, Keller, and Srinivasan, 2002.

Anwar Sadat government rolled back the price increase, as it feared that the riots might result in its downfall.

Not every price increase has been followed by riots. In fact, prices of subsidized commodities have been raised thousands of times over the years. Such factors as the overall state of the economy, the size of the price increase, the popularity of the government, public information campaigns, and the provision of offsetting benefits, such as increases in the minimum wage or government salaries, significantly affect the likelihood of sustained popular opposition to price increases. Governments in the region, wishing to stay in power, have attempted to learn these lessons and make adjustments in subsidy programs in the most–socially palatable ways possible.

Despite these political concerns, the fiscal costs of food and fuel subsidies have become so large that governments of the energy poor have been forced to take action. Fiscal pressures in Algeria, Jordan, and Morocco forced these governments to modify their subsidy programs. However, there are important holdouts, with Egypt perhaps the most prominent example. Subsidies accounted for 35 percent of Egypt's 2008–2009 fiscal year budget, with nearly half of those subsidies used to hold down prices of energy.[25]

The governments of the energy poor have generally adopted one of two courses of action. The first has involved reducing the number of subsidized items while maintaining universal access to those items that remained subsidized. In some instances, the reduction in the number of subsidized items has been accompanied by price increases as well; in other instances, prices on the remaining subsidized items stay unchanged. These changes in food-subsidy programs have reduced fiscal costs, sometimes at the expense of the poor. In Algeria, price increases on foodstuffs were followed by sharp declines in food consumption by the very poor.[26] The second approach is to attempt to target subsidies by restricting them to the poor through some form of means testing, such as providing ration cards to families that give proof of low incomes.

These measures frequently fail to eliminate the most-pernicious effects of subsidies. To the extent to which governments merely raise prices but continue to employ price controls and provide universal subsidies, they might inherit the worst of all worlds. In the public eye, the government, not market forces, is blamed for the price increase. Because the government is responsible for the prices of these goods, consumers seek to change government behavior rather than their own when prices are raised, often resorting to demonstrations and strikes. Continued government controls forestall market responses that might improve the long-run supply of these goods. Arab governments have frequently found it convenient to control the supply chain in order to control prices more effectively. However, the large state-owned trading and supply companies that have been set up to distribute food and fuel usually have little incentive to improve efficiency or alter their operations. Consumers see little in the way of better provision after prices rise. More-substantial policy changes—most notably, price liberalization and opening up the sector to competition—are needed to elicit supply-side responses that will raise overall levels of output and welfare.

Reducing Barriers to Entry. Arab businesses often complain vociferously about the environment in which they operate. In response to these complaints, most of the governments of the energy poor now pay lip service to improving the climate for business. However, improving

---

[25] Abdel-Razek, 2008.

[26] World Bank, 1999, p. 14.

the business environment is closely tied to reducing corruption, and the major causes of corruption are complicated government rules, regulations, and taxes and the bureaucracy used to enforce them. Some of the easiest reforms have been in the area of business registration. Governments have reasserted control over the bureaucracy by insisting on streamlining and easing registration procedures. Some governments have relaxed overly strict labor laws: International experience suggests that, when layoffs and dismissals become too expensive, businesses refrain from hiring. Morocco has changed labor market policies to encourage employment of nationals. However, all the governments in the region have been reluctant to tackle the problem of overstaffing in government bureaucracies. Aside from the high fiscal costs of paying civil servants without enough to do, the large bureaucracies continue to invent ways of impeding legitimate business activities so as to be able to request bribes.

Trade Liberalization and Exchange Rate Policies. In contrast to the energy rich, the energy poor do not pump most of their exports out of the ground. They have to compete with the rest of the world for the sale of manufactures and agricultural products to pay for imports of food, raw materials, and consumer and investment goods. Policies, domestic and foreign, have major effects on export performance. Those countries that have implemented more-open trade and commercial economic policies have experienced stronger export growth.

A number of these governments have focused on reducing external barriers to exports. Most of the energy poor have signed association agreements with the EU. These provide favorable—in many cases, duty-free—access, to EU markets. The United States has also signed free-trade agreements with Jordan and Morocco and grants the same status to the West Bank and Gaza. All the better-performing exporters have preferred trade access to the EU or the United States. In addition to these agreements with major trading partners, a number of the energy poor have taken initiatives to reduce barriers to interregional trade. In February 2004, Egypt, Jordan, Morocco, and Tunisia signed an agreement as an initial step toward the creation of a Euro-Mediterranean free-trade area by 2010.[27]

However, taking steps to reduce external barriers to trade is not enough. *Domestic barriers* to trade generally have a greater impact on exports than foreign barriers have. Policy success in creating a more-favorable climate for exports has often been stalled by half-measures. For example, Jordan, Morocco, and Tunisia have all liberalized trade and financial markets, although with mixed success. In both Morocco and Tunisia, even though most trade now takes place with partners in free-trade agreements, the remaining hodgepodge of tariffs and trade restrictions makes trade with nonpreferential partners unduly difficult. Tunisia has made it possible for offshore companies to set up export operations exempt from import tariffs and quotas. These companies have created a dynamic export enclave that stitches clothing and shoes for European and U.S. markets. Although useful, the rest of the economy remains isolated from the dynamic export zones. Exporters procure components and raw materials abroad, employ local labor, then reexport the product. Linkages between domestic suppliers and exporters fail to materialize. Furthermore, the light taxation regimes for exporters in these zones shift the tax burden onto domestic producers that might be less profitable and less able to pay.

A key stimulus to exports is exchange rate markets. If manufacturers can easily purchase the foreign currency they need to pay for inputs, they are able to expand output and exports

---

[27] Agénor et al., 2004, p. 16. At the time of publication, the EuroMed Free Trade Area has yet to be established.

when opportunities arise. In fact, market participants' ability to freely buy and sell foreign exchange is as important as how the exchange rate is set.

Most of the energy poor have liberalized their exchange rate regimes in recent years. The Egyptian government, which had a preference for multitier exchange rate regimes and the accompanying controls, has unified the exchange rate, beginning with a series of steps in 1992. The process of liberalization has brought the exchange rate down to levels consistent with market forces as the Egyptian pound depreciated by 40 percent between 2000 and mid-year 2004. The combination of a more-liberal exchange rate regime and a more-competitive rate resulted in substantial growth in exports of both goods and services, especially tourism, and a concomitant acceleration of growth in GDP.[28] With the exception of Syria, the other countries in this group have also pursued more-liberal foreign exchange regimes. The policy changes have been accompanied by an acceleration in export growth.

Privatization and Financial-Sector Reform. Until the 1990s, *privatization* was a dirty word in the Arab world. Even now, moves to privatize have been more hesitant in this region than in Latin America and Asia, not to mention Central and Eastern Europe. Jordan and, more recently, Egypt and Morocco have moved most aggressively. As part of a massive shift in economic policy following the first Gulf War, stimulated by creditors' commitments to write down its foreign debt, Egypt reluctantly began to privatize in the 1990s. It sold 130 enterprises in 1994 and 1995, valued at $3.8 billion.[29] After a marked slowdown in privatization in the second half of the 1990s, privatization has taken off in this decade with sales of the Bank of Alexandria and state-owned shares in joint venture banks. Jordan, Lebanon, Morocco, and Tunisia had smaller public sectors. Sales of banks, manufacturing plants, telecommunication companies and licenses, and other assets have proceeded. However, the state still operates a number of large enterprises in both Morocco and Tunisia. In all cases, the easy privatizations involved assets or companies that could be sold for substantial sums of money or smaller businesses that could be easily sold to local businesses. Governments have not privatized utilities in water and electric power or oil and gas companies.

What Is the Outlook for Economic Growth in the Energy-Poor Countries?

Like most of the energy rich, the energy poor are suffering from the global recession but, for the most part, are projected to continue to grow. As of this writing, of the energy poor, only Lebanon and Yemen have borrowed from the IMF. Exports, remittances, and incomes from tourism have fallen, but lower commodity prices, especially for food and petroleum products, have led to improvements in terms of trade in some countries and eased pressures on the poor. With some luck, these countries could see a return to growth rates of the recent past by 2011.

As in the previous chapter, we compare potential growth in per capita GDP in the energy rich for 2010 to 2020 under two scenarios. In the first scenario, GDP is assumed to grow at the average rate enjoyed by the country between 2000 and 2008. In the second scenario, growth proceeds at the average rates from 1990 to 2000. In both scenarios, per capita GDP is calculated by dividing projected GDP by population as forecast by the U.S. Census Bureau. As in the previous chapter, the purpose of the exercise is not to project future growth rates but to illustrate potential improvements in growth in per capita incomes.

---

[28] IMF, "IMF Concludes 2004 Article IV Consultation with the Arab Republic of Egypt," public information notice 04/69, July 12, 2004d.

[29] World Bank, 2001, p. 16.

Figure 4.9 (the counterpart to Figure 3.12 in Chapter Three) compares average annual increases in per capita GDP for these two scenarios. In contrast to the energy rich, not all of the energy poor have enjoyed substantially more-rapid economic growth between 2000 and 2008 than between 1990 and 2000. While growth has been substantially more rapid in Jordan, Lebanon, and Morocco, it has been about the same in Egypt, Syria, and Tunisia, and slower in Yemen. Higher prices for oil and gas were the primary reason for the unilaterally better performance in the latter period for the energy rich. For the energy poor, differences in performance reflect differences in the structures of the individual economies and the dates on which economic policy changes were made. For example, Egypt enjoyed a surge in growth in the 1990s because of massive debt relief, more-liberal economic policies, and better fiscal balance; growth slowed slightly between 2000 and 2008 as some of the fruits of the initial liberalization measures had been reaped. In contrast, improvements in this decade in security and the political situation in Jordan and Lebanon have contributed to more-rapid growth in those two countries.

In either event, if growth continues at the rates of the recent past, the energy poor will enjoy appreciable increases in per capita incomes. Between 2010 and 2020, per capita GDP would rise at average annual rates ranging from 3.0 percent per annum in the case of Egypt to 4.5 percent in the case of Jordan. By 2020, per capita GDP would be 34 to 55 percent higher than in 2010 in these countries, an appreciable difference. The only exception would be Yemen, the poorest in the group. Because of continued rapid rates of population growth, if Yemen continues to grow at recent rates of 4.4 percent per year, per capita incomes will rise slowly, barely increasing by 10 percent over the coming decade.

How likely is it that these rates of economic growth will resume? Egypt, Jordan, Morocco, and Tunisia have made significant moves toward liberalizing their economies, especially trade, in the past decade. Free-trade agreements with the EU and the United States have helped spur

Figure 4.9

Change in Per Capita GDP in the Energy Rich Between 2010 and 2020, Using Average Growth Rates of the 1990s and 2000–2008

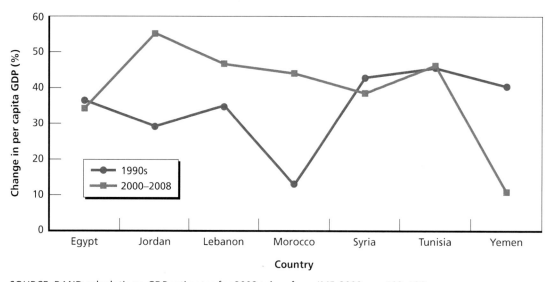

SOURCE: RAND calculations. GDP estimates for 2008 taken from IMF, 2009, pp. 193–195.
RAND TR912-4.9

this development. Some progress has been made on liberalizing controlled prices on refined oil products and food and better targeting food and other subsidies. A number of formerly state-owned companies have been privatized. The energy poor have also attempted to make their local business climates more hospitable for private entrepreneurs.

However, to make further progress in reducing barriers to entry for new businesses and to foster private-sector job creation, the governments will need to markedly improve the efficiency of their bureaucracies and social welfare systems. Making the bureaucracy more efficient not only will entail streamlining procedures but will also involve reducing staffs and linking rewards to performance. Because of the entrenched opposition of the bureaucracy, implementing these changes will be difficult. Despite some reforms, the governments preserve expensive, often dysfunctional systems of subsidies. Making further changes in these systems might well be politically dangerous. In short, building on past measures to make these economies more efficient should help sustain growth, but, outside of privatization, additional changes in policies to accelerate growth might not be implemented.

Institutional reform will not be the sole factor determining economic growth. For most of the energy poor, security, internal and external, will remain a more-important determinant of growth than economic policy. As shown by the recent events in the region, countries suffer economically from conflict, either domestic or from spillover effects from neighboring states. Countries suffer substantial economic losses from unrest and conflict, especially from falloffs in tourism revenues. If security remains a major problem, economic growth will suffer. For example, Egypt and Tunisua experienced falloffs in tourism revenues from their unrest.

Labor Markets of the Energy-Poor Countries

No other economic issue is deemed as important to the stability of the Arab world as growth in employment and real wages. The region continues to undergo rapid growth in its labor force, even as overall rates of population growth have moderated. During the 1990s, rapid growth in the labor force took place at a time of modest increases in output. As a consequence, real wages fell or stagnated in many countries. Fiscal stringencies forced governments to limit and, in some cases, reduce public-sector employment, the sector in which many have traditionally sought work. In this decade, increased demand for expatriate Arab labor from the energy rich coupled with better domestic economic performance from the energy poor have created a better environment for employment and wage growth. However, it is not clear whether this will be sustained in the decades ahead. The success with which the region generates more jobs and increases in incomes will have a crucial effect on the direction and extent of pressure for political change.

In this section, we explore employment and unemployment in the energy-poor countries and pressures for change and alternative policies.

Employment in the Energy-Poor Countries

Migrant Labor. The most-striking differences between labor markets in the energy rich and the energy poor are the roles of foreign labor and the small-scale private sector. In contrast to the energy rich, the energy poor export, not import, labor. During the 1970s and 1980s, they provided the workers who constructed the new homes, highways, and ports in the Persian Gulf states, Iraq, and Libya. They also ran the hospitals and staffed the schools. The most-important exporters of labor were Egypt, the two (now one) Yemens, and Palestinians, primarily with Jordanian identity papers.

Labor has not only flowed from one Arab state to another. As recently as 1992, Israel employed 120,000 Palestinians in Israel proper and the settlements, about one-fifth of the Palestinian workforce in that year.[30] The Maghreb states, energy rich and poor alike, have exported labor to Europe. Over half a million Algerians and even more Moroccans are working in France legally; many more when illegal immigrants are included. More than 1.5 million Moroccans have legally emigrated to the EU, 4.6 percent of Morocco's total population. A substantial share of the Tunisian workforce also works in Europe.

The end of the oil boom had deleterious consequences for expatriate laborers from the energy poor. The Yemenis and Palestinians suffered the most. The loss of jobs in the Saudi construction industry in the late 1980s followed by the expulsion of Yemeni workers in the aftermath of the first Gulf War wrought havoc with Yemen's economy. Per capita gross national income, which includes remittances, plummeted; it is still far lower today than in the early 1980s. Jordan experienced a rise in its unemployment rate to 19 percent in 1991, after Kuwait expelled Palestinian workers following the Gulf War.[31]

While the 1990–1991 Gulf War convinced the energy-rich states that expatriate labor drawn from the non-Arab countries of South Asia and the Philippines was politically safer than their Arab counterparts, recent events have demonstrated the potential for labor unrest among these labor pools as well. Difficult working conditions combined with the corrosive effect of inflation on real wages have led to labor strikes by Indian workers in both the UAE and Bahrain.[32] In Kuwait, Bangladeshi workers recently picketed for higher wages, prompting a round of deportations.

The Small-Scale Private Urban Sector. The second major difference between labor markets in the energy rich and those in the energy poor is the role of small-scale businesses and itinerant work in providing employment. Activities include maid services, street vending, trucking, taxis, and laundry services. These activities are the most-important source of urban employment in the energy-poor states. Estimates of the numbers of urban members of the workforce employed in these activities range from 42 percent in Syria to 55 percent in Egypt.[33] These numbers are not extraordinarily high by developing-country standards: In much of the developing world, these activities account for higher shares of economic activity.

Employment in these activities is much more precarious than in the state sector. Most work is paid by the job or service rendered: In Iraq, day laborers who work in warehouses might be paid by the sackload. Incomes depend much more on the level of economic activity than in salaried jobs. During good times, both the amount of work and money paid rise; during hard times, they both fall. Thus, from the point of view of financial security, job seekers prefer public-sector jobs.

Agriculture. Agriculture still looms large in the energy poor, especially in terms of employment. In Morocco, 55 percent of the workforce is engaged in agriculture. Agriculture is the

---

[30] Ishac Diwan and Radwan `Ali Sha`ban, *Development Under Adversity: The Palestinian Economy in Transition*, Washington, D.C.: World Bank, March 1999.

[31] Richards and Waterbury, 1996, p. 396.

[32] Roger Hardy, "Migrants Demand Labour Rights in Gulf," *BBC News*, February 27, 2008.

[33] Agénor et al., 2004, p. 5.

most-important employer in Egypt and Yemen as well. More than half the population of these two countries lives in the countryside. Among the energy poor, only Lebanon is as urbanized as the energy rich, and only in Jordan does agriculture play as small a role in the economy.

In contrast, outside of Iraq and Algeria, agriculture is not an important part of the economies of the energy rich, accounting for a tiny fraction of GDP (Figure 4.10). Moreover, a much smaller share of the population lives in rural areas in the energy rich than in the energy poor. Except for Algeria, in the energy-rich countries, two-thirds or more of inhabitants live in cities.

Agriculture and other predominantly rural occupations are the employers of last resort in the energy poor; they provide the safety valve for the job market. To fulfill that role, agricultural wages have had to remain flexible, rising and falling with fluctuations in supply and demand, especially supply. During the oil-boom years, rural laborers flocked to Saudi Arabia from Egypt and Yemen, where they could earn several times the prevailing wages at home. The exodus of labor pushed up local farm wages; when the good times ended, local wages fell.[34] Because agriculture is the residual employer, productivity and wages tend to be lower than in urban areas. Not surprisingly, the incidence of poverty in the Arab world is much higher in the countryside than in the cities.[35]

State Employment in the Energy-Poor Countries. As in the energy rich, governments are an important employer among the energy poor and the major employer in the formal sector of the economy.[36] As in the energy rich, there are relatively few large incorporated private businesses, domestic or foreign, in the region that would provide stable salaries and employment conditions comparable with government bureaucracies or state-owned companies.

Figure 4.10
The Role of Agriculture in the Arab World

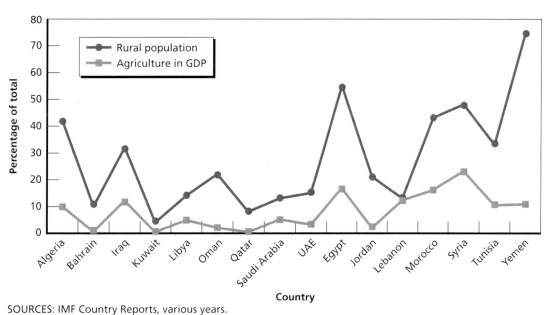

SOURCES: IMF Country Reports, various years.
RAND *TR912-4.10*

***

[34] Richards and Waterbury, 1996, pp. 369, 377.

[35] World Bank, 2001, p. 7.

[36] Agénor et al., 2004, p. 5.

Also as in the energy-rich countries, the state's inordinate role in providing formal employment is among the major causes of these economies' poor performance in terms of improving productivity and, hence, slow economic growth. In Egypt, the government employs roughly one out of four people in the formal economy. The large, inefficient civil service has become a major barrier to economic policy changes and improvements in productivity. Surplus public-sector employees not only burden the budget; they intensely oppose efforts to reform the civil service, such as making staff more accountable, reducing overall staffing, or limiting administrative discretion that helps to create opportunities for soliciting bribes.[37]

State-owned companies have also been a drag on growth. For example, state ownership of utilities has resulted in high costs, poor service, and inefficient utilization of capital in the energy poor and energy rich alike. Because the supply of electricity, water, sewage, and transportation infrastructure, such as roads, public transport, ports, and airports, is crucial for other economic activities, poor performance in these sectors raises the costs of doing business, retarding growth in incomes and economic activity.[38] State ownership in these sectors crowds out private-sector investment because state-owned companies have preferential access to loans and other sources of investment and government subsidies. State-owned companies also benefit from government prohibitions on competition from private-sector providers.

The state tends to distort labor markets by paying above-market wages, financed by taxes on productive activities. Civil service wages often serve as reference points for wages in publicly owned companies and even in the few large private-sector companies that exist in the energy poor. As a consequence, employment in the small private sector of the formal economy is often constrained by government wage policies.[39] The size of the state wage bill has also had negative effects on economic growth. In Tunisia, for example, the state wage bill has exceeded 12 percent of GDP and has crowded out government expenditures on infrastructure investment and other public goods.[40] Because the wage bill has to be financed from taxes on other economic activities, to the extent that the civil service and state-owned companies are overstaffed, resources needed elsewhere are squandered.

Unemployment

Because of the importance of agriculture and small-scale businesses in urban areas in employment in the energy poor, defining and measuring unemployment is a tricky task in these countries. Figure 4.11 shows unemployment rates for several countries in the region based on the methodologies used by the International Labour Organization (ILO). These numbers are based on household surveys in which household members of working age are asked whether they were without work, wanted to work, and were actively seeking work. If the respondents answer no to any of these questions, they are not considered unemployed. An individual is classified as employed if he or she worked any time in the previous period. Consequently, employment does not imply that laborers punch a clock and work a 40-hour week. Substantial parts of the day might be spent looking for jobs or waiting for customers in the bazaar or on the roadside. Although time spent in this fashion might not be very productive, waiting in a booth

---

[37] World Bank, 2001, p. 7.

[38] World Bank, 2001, Annex 1, p. 5.

[39] Agénor et al., 2004, p. 7.

[40] IMF, 2003a, p. 16.

Figure 4.11
Unemployment Rates in the Energy Poor

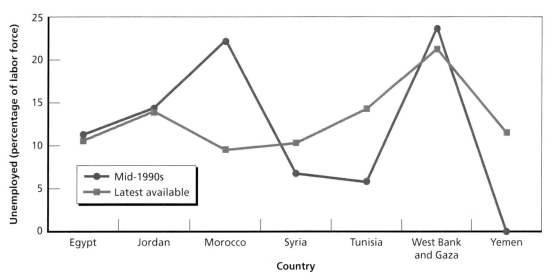

SOURCES: ILO; World Bank.
NOTE: Data listed are 2007 for Jordan, Morocco, and the West Bank and Gaza; 2006 for Egypt and Tunisia; 2003 for Syria; and 1999 for Yemen.
RAND *TR912-4.11*

at a market for customers is still work. In fact, many stall owners in the Arab world put in very long hours to earn their livings. Climatic conditions also serve to encourage irregular working hours. During very hot months, laborers often work only mornings because of the heat. In agriculture, work is often seasonal: During planting and harvest, families work around the clock; during other periods, the work tempo is more relaxed.

Because work in the formal economy tends to be hourly while that in agriculture and small businesses is less tied to a clock, perceptions and alternative measures of unemployment tend to vary widely. For example, the Central Statistical Organization of Iraq (now the Central Organization for Statistics and Information Technology) found that the unemployment rate ran 17.6 percent in the summer of 2006,[41] but Iraqi ministers and U.S. government officials frequently cite unsubstantiated rates of 40 to 50 percent. The higher rates reflected perceptions or the belief that "real" jobs are only those involving a regular salary, i.e., in the public sector (as opposed to, say, day agricultural labor). Similar discrepancies between the unemployment rates published by the national statistical offices and rates mentioned in the press occur frequently throughout the region. From an economic perspective, the ILO rates are most meaningful because they reflect the economic activities undertaken by people, not the numbers of jobs that fit a narrow definition of what constitutes employment.

Because of the low unemployment rates in the Gulf states, unemployment rates tend to be higher in the energy poor than in the energy rich. Unemployment rates in the energy poor are still substantially higher on average than in other developing regions, such as Africa, Latin America, and East Asia.[42] Unemployment rates in the energy poor tend to be higher for the

---

[41] Unemployment in 2006 for Iraqis ages 15 and older was 17.5 percent of the labor force (Central Organization for Statistics and Information Technology, *Unemployment Survey 2006*).

[42] ILO, 2002, p. 16.

better educated than for the unskilled. The unskilled appear willing to settle for lower wages and work while the better educated sometimes wait for a better-paying (government) job.[43] As in the energy rich, the influx of new entrants to the labor market has contributed to higher unemployment rates in a number of countries. Unemployment rates for new entrants are much higher than for older workers. Urban unemployment rates are higher than rural rates.

Pressures for Change and Alternative Policies

As increasing numbers of young people have entered the labor force in recent years, the role of the state as the primary employer has become untenable. Both the World Bank and the IMF argue that the distortions and productivity losses associated with such large state sectors have been detrimental to economic growth and have served, on a net basis, to reduce employment opportunities and real incomes. If growth is to accelerate in these countries, productivity in the state sector will have to rise. In many countries, this will necessitate a reduction or, at a minimum, stagnation in state-sector employment.

This will not be an easy task. No other policy measure has been resisted so tenaciously as reducing state-sector employment. Opposition to such a policy shift is widespread. Because so many people are employed by the state, the constituency in support of state employment is large, especially in the politically important urban areas. Opposition does not just emanate from civil servants. Because state salaries are often the only steady source of income for extended families, aunts, uncles, cousins, and other family members also oppose change. Recent graduates also oppose reductions in state employment, because such measures serve to dash their own hopes for future state-sector employment. Ministers oppose reductions in staffing levels because such moves undercut their authority and ability to provide patronage by dispensing jobs. Consequently, senior policymakers throughout the region have generally failed to reduce staffing.

Despite these political hurdles, as noted earlier, fiscal pressures are forcing change. The state wage bill is so high in a number of energy-poor states that government expenditures on public services and investment have been curtailed.[44] Governments have responded by wage and hiring freezes. The former has resulted in a number of disgruntled and sometimes even less productive civil servants. The latter has had marginal success in preventing further growth in state-sector employment.

Privatization has had more success in reducing state-sector employment and improving productivity. Once a state-owned company has private owners, the new owners have the authority to reduce staffing and change salary structures—measures that the state is unwilling to take. By transferring ownership, the state also transfers the problems of downsizing and improving productivity to groups that have a profit incentive to make these changes. None-theless, Arab countries have generally been reluctant privatizers. Whereas many citizens of the former Soviet bloc, India, and China have become fed up with state ownership of enterprises, the remnants of Nasserite socialist ideology, fears of Western multinationals, and suspicions that privatization will be just another way by which government ministers will be able to line their pockets have left the public less than enthusiastic about privatization. Many government

---

[43] Richards and Waterbury, 1996, p. 134.

[44] IMF, 2003a, p. 15.

officials, concerned about losing access to jobs, cash, and contracts, have ardently opposed privatization as well.

Despite the opposition, there has been some progress, especially in this decade. Government decisions to privatize have been driven by the same practical factors that have driven privatizations in the rest of the world: the need for cash to cover government budget deficits and the imperative to reduce losses generated by state-owned enterprises. Continued privatization provides one of the more-fruitful avenues for increasing productivity and accelerating economic growth in the region.

As for the future, under conditions of a return to economic growth rates of the recent past, the outlook for the labor market is modestly positive. Rates of unemployment have dropped sharply in Algeria, Morocco, and a few other Arab countries in recent years. Privatization of state-owned enterprises has increased labor productivity and, counterintuitively, employment, by lowering the cost of business services and making the labor market more flexible. But governments in the region still impose strictures on firing, hiring, and minimum wages that have discouraged businesses from hiring and entrepreneurs from investing. Additional measures to improve labor market flexibility and a shift in social acceptance of female participation in the labor force are likely to increase employment and accelerate growth. In all but Yemen, growth rates should be rapid enough that real wages will rise along with employment.

CHAPTER FIVE

Conclusions and Implications for U.S. Policymakers

In this chapter, we summarize some of the key conclusions from the demographic and economic analyses and present some implications of those conclusions for U.S. policymakers.

Demographic Trends: Conclusions and Implications

Conclusions About Demographic Trends

Over the next decade, the rapid pace of population growth in the Arab world will continue to slow, but the numbers of young people entering the labor force will continue to rise. These young people are better educated but have higher aspirations than previous generations. Yet, a traditional source of jobs, the government, has stopped or slowed hiring in most of these countries. The desire for work coupled with a decline in opportunities in government, the most–sought-after sector, creates a potentially explosive disconnect between societal expectations and government capacity. Whether the influx of better-educated young people into the workforce will be a force of rapid transformation of Arab societies along reformist lines or a source of instability is the key question. Two trends in where these young people will live and work will have a major effect on stability in the region.

A Region of Cities. The Arab world is one of the world's most-urbanized developing regions. Unlike other parts of the developing world, where the movement of population from the countryside to the cities is a relatively recent phenomenon, the Arab region has been defined by its cities for millennia. Over the past several decades, Arab cities have grown rapidly. Initially, this growth was concentrated in the capital cities, but, more recently, regional centers have experienced the most-rapid growth. The expansion of the region's cities will reinforce the social, political, economic, and security challenges that Arab regimes face. How these cities develop will be integral to the future of Arab societies and will be an important avenue for Western engagement.

Under conditions of rapid growth and large numbers of job seekers, cities will be cockpits for social unrest and political change. As shown by recent events, unbridled urbanization is likely to fuel an already explosive mixture of social discontent because of the proximity of rival ethnic and religious groups within Arab cities (Baghdad and Beirut offer good examples), the erosion of social restraints, and the anonymity conferred by urban areas. Cities are likely to be the leading theater for political violence and terrorism, especially terrorism that aims at a national and global audience.

Movements aiming to overthrow or consolidate political power will find their center of gravity in cities. Moderate Islamist oppositions will, as in the past, find opportunities to dem-

79

onstrate their social-welfare and good-governance credentials in urban settings. The success of economic reforms will be largely measured by increases in economic activity in and around cities. Conversely, the failure of dysfunctional regimes is most evident and most consequential in cities, including the second-tier cities that are beginning to experience the same stresses associated with the region's capitals.

Many of the high-leverage opportunities for Western influence, through diplomacy, academic and other exchanges, investment, and trade, on the region's political and economic evolution will be found in urban settings. In particular, Western policy goals of reducing support for terrorist groups and improving popular perceptions of Western countries, especially the United States, need to be pursued in the cities. In such countries as Egypt, Morocco, and Yemen, this might well imply a reorientation of development efforts from the poorest of the poor, who still tend to live in rural areas, to richer but more-volatile urban areas.

A Region of Migrants. The Arab world has long been affected by migration. People from all social classes and religious persuasions emigrate—in most cases, spurred by the desire for better economic prospects but sometimes as a lifestyle choice for middle-class citizens. Western practices might be adopted or rejected, but Arab societies are not indifferent to or unaffected by this growing transnationalism. The large numbers of Arabs residing in Europe and the United States are a very tangible link to new ways of thinking about government and the economy. For many migrants, residence in the West is also a source of alienation and, in some cases, radicalization. This phenomenon, evident in the extensive network of al Qaeda–linked cells in Western Europe, shows few signs of reversal, despite tighter immigration and internal security policies. In fact, declining populations of working adults in Europe coupled with rapid growth in the numbers of young Arabs looking for work ensure that migration from the Arab world to Europe and, to a lesser extent, the United States will continue over the next decade despite attempts to constrain immigration.

The Arab immigrant communities abroad have emerged in both positive and negative ways as leading vehicles for change in the region itself. These communities will be a key variable to watch over the next decade. It might not be an exaggeration to say that the future of the Arab world, especially those areas, such as the Maghreb, that are in particularly close contact with the West, will be shaped as much by developments in Paris, Frankfurt, or even Dearborn as by developments in the region itself. To the extent that young Arabs in the West become more embedded and committed to Western societies and face less discrimination in the workplace and in looking for housing, the more likely this community is to become a force for combating rather than supporting terrorist groups.

Implications That Demographic Trends Might Have for U.S. Policy

Although fertility rates and population growth rates have been declining, the population of the Arab world is still growing more rapidly than those of other parts of the world. Increasing populations are straining water resources, public services, and infrastructure. However, fertility rates are not uniform: Some Arab countries have much higher fertility rates than others. Slower rates of population growth would ease pressures on water supplies and on governments to provide more public services, especially in countries with rapid rates of population growth. Over time, slower rates of population growth would permit Arab governments to shift from focusing on quantity to improving quality.

U.S. assistance programs can help ease these pressures by continuing to support family planning initiatives across the region, especially in countries that have higher fertility rates.

More U.S. funding to train local staff to conduct outreach and to make contraceptives more widely available would be valuable, as would more indirectly supporting female education. Given the sensitivities of family planning among some religious conservatives in the region, the United States should take pains to build off of local initiatives and, to the extent possible, keep local organizations as the "face" of these programs and the primary interface with communities.

Policy toward Arab migrants resident—or attempting to reside—in the United States and Europe will be an increasingly important factor influencing their host-government policies toward the Arab and the Muslim worlds. Policies in these traditionally distinct areas will be more difficult to pursue in isolation, despite the clear intellectual and bureaucratic obstacles to integration. At a minimum, policymakers should recognize that Arab and Muslim communities abroad are now a critical part of the equation and will provide an increasingly important window into political futures in the region itself. They are a valuable point of engagement, from counterterrorism to political and economic reform. The special prominence of Muslim communities and political networks in Europe and their close connection to developments in North Africa and elsewhere also mean that there is a strong argument to be made for transatlantic coordination in this as in many other facets of U.S. strategy vis-à-vis the Arab world.

In this regard, the implementation of procedures to provide tourist, student, and business visas to the United States can have major effects on U.S. influence in the region. The large numbers of Arabs who have studied, lived, and worked in the United States have been a major source of U.S. influence in the region. These individuals serve as natural bridges between the United States and the Arab world, and many go on to be decisionmakers or opinion leaders in their countries of origin. The sharp decline in the numbers of Arab students studying in the United States following September 11 because of more stringent visa regulations has been detrimental to U.S. interests. Procedures for obtaining visas and entering the United States that are perceived as disrespectful also harm U.S. interests. The U.S. government should carefully review current procedures to ensure that they both prevent the entry of individuals seeking to harm the United States and, simultaneously, ensure that Arabs seeking to visit the United States to study, visit, or conduct business are treated with respect and are able to obtain visas in a timely, efficient manner.

Economic Trends: Conclusions and Implications

Conclusions About Economic Trends

Energy Rich. For the foreseeable future, the world will continue to depend on oil pumped from the Arab region, especially the Persian Gulf. The region will continue to account for one-third of global production in 2020. Even if rates of depletion are higher than previously estimated and production costs in the Persian Gulf double or triple their current levels of just a few dollars per barrel, the Gulf states will remain the world's lowest-cost producers. They will hold more than half of global reserves.

Despite their oil riches, the energy-rich countries in the region fell on hard times after the oil boom of the 1970s ended. In most countries in the Gulf, per capita GDP in constant-dollar terms is still below previous peaks. The primary reason for the poor economic performance of these larger countries has been declines in factor productivity. These declines have been due to poor investment decisions and microeconomic policies, especially price subsidies and bureaucratic barriers to the entry of new firms into markets.

Economic output in the energy rich, especially for the smaller Gulf states, will continue to be closely linked to oil output and prices. However, oil and gas exports will serve more as a foundation than a driver of growth. Only in Iraq are increases in oil production likely to appreciably exceed population growth through 2020. Although energy will continue to provide a ready source of revenues for governments, the key to increasing per capita incomes will be increasing factor productivity.

To increase factor productivity, these countries need to reduce price distortions by cutting producer and, to the extent politically feasible, consumer price subsidies. Barriers to trade and foreign investment need to be reduced, especially in Algeria and Libya. Continued expansion and integration of the GCC would do much to increase competition and improve factor productivity in those countries. Privatization of non–energy-sector assets has improved efficiency and generated more-rapid growth in revenues and output of formerly state-owned enterprises in those Arab countries that have braved this step. A more-aggressive approach to privatization would generate additional benefits in terms of accelerated growth in factor productivity.

How likely are the governments of the energy-rich countries to adopt policies that would foster more-efficient use of resources? Going forward, we expect the GCC countries to continue to push ahead with economic liberalization, regional integration, and privatization. If oil prices continue to stay substantially higher than their average levels of the 1990s, the citizens of the smaller countries should continue to enjoy high levels of incomes and continued growth. Algeria, Iraq, Libya, and, to a lesser extent, Saudi Arabia pose more-difficult challenges. They are poorer, have larger populations, and are more vulnerable to political unrest. Further liberalization in the first three countries is likely to be slow.

None of the energy rich has successfully addressed the issue of state employment. These governments will need to devise incentives to encourage new entrants to the labor force to seek jobs outside of government. Modest shifts in expectations have taken place in some of these countries, as jobs in private finance and some service industries have become socially acceptable, but the government overwhelmingly remains the preferred employer. In light of the political difficulties, we do not expect these states to cut employment of nationals in overstaffed state bureaucracies or state-controlled companies.

Energy Poor. Improvements in economic policies from unifying exchange rates, reducing tariffs and other barriers to trade, and privatization have contributed to more-rapid growth in all but one of the energy poor over the past two decades than was the case in the 1980s. In most instances, higher oil prices have also helped the energy poor as demand for foreign labor has risen in the Gulf, leading to increased remittances and, in the case of Egypt and Syria, bumped up the value of their own modest exports of oil and natural gas.

Like most of the energy rich, the energy poor are suffering from the global recession, but, for the most part, their economies are projected to continue to grow. Exports, remittances, and incomes from tourism are falling, but lower commodity prices, especially for food and petroleum products, have eased pressures on the poor. With some luck, these countries could see a return to growth rates of the recent past by 2011. If growth recovers to the rates of the recent past, the energy poor will enjoy appreciable increases in per capita incomes through 2020, with per capita GDP rising by 3.0 percent per annum in the case of Egypt and 4.5 percent in the case of Jordan because solid growth in GDP is accompanied by slower rates of growth in population.

How likely is it that these rates of economic growth will resume? Egypt, Jordan, Morocco, and Tunisia have made significant moves toward liberalizing their economies, especially trade, over the past decade. Free-trade agreements with the EU and the United States have helped spur this development. Some progress has been made on liberalizing controlled prices on refined oil products and food and on better targeting food and other subsidies. A number of formerly state-owned companies have been privatized. The energy poor have also attempted to make their local business climates more hospitable for private entrepreneurs.

To make further progress in reducing barriers to entry for new businesses and to foster private-sector job creation, the governments will need to markedly improve the efficiency of their bureaucracies and social welfare systems. Making the bureaucracy more efficient will not only entail streamlining procedures but will also involve cutting staffs and linking rewards to performance. Because of the entrenched opposition of the bureaucracy, implementing these changes will be difficult. In addition, despite some reforms, these governments preserve expensive, often dysfunctional systems of subsidies. Making further changes in these systems is likely to be politically difficult.

Under conditions of a return to past growth rates, the outlook for growth in employment and wages is modestly positive. Rates of unemployment have dropped sharply in Algeria, Morocco, and a few other Arab countries in recent years. Privatization of state-owned enterprises has increased labor productivity and, counterintuitively, employment, by lowering the cost of business services and making the labor market more flexible. But governments in the region still impose strictures on firing, hiring, and minimum wages that have discouraged businesses from hiring and entrepreneurs from investing. Additional measures to improve labor market flexibility and a shift in social acceptance of female participation in the labor force are likely to increase employment and accelerate growth. In all but Yemen, growth rates should be rapid enough that workers' real wages will rise along with employment.

Institutional reform will not be the sole factor determining economic growth. For most of the energy poor, security, internal and external, will remain the key determinant of growth. As shown by the recent events in the region, countries suffer economically from conflict, either domestic or from spillover effects from neighboring states. Countries suffer substantial economic losses from unrest and conflict, especially from falloffs in tourism revenues. If security remains a major problem, economic growth will suffer. For example, Egypt and Tunisia experienced falloffs in tourism revenues from their unrest.

Implications That Economic Trends Might Have for U.S. Policy

Energy Rich. Outside of Iraq, the U.S. government does not have much in the way of economic leverage with the energy-rich states of the Arab world. Because these countries do not receive substantial economic assistance from the United States, the U.S. government will need to encourage these countries to continue to reduce barriers to trade and the operations of businesses, domestic and foreign, through suasion or indirectly through other institutions. The United States should work through the G-20 to encourage Saudi Arabia to open up its economy more broadly and to pursue continued integration through the GCC.

Oil output and prices have impinged on U.S. relations with the energy rich, especially Saudi Arabia. Outside of discussions with these governments concerning broader roles for foreign, including U.S., companies, in their energy industries, we believe that the U.S. government should relegate discussions about oil output and markets to low levels. In our view, high-level discussions about oil output and prices muddy other U.S. messages about economic policies. These discussions might also give the governments of the energy rich an exaggerated sense of the importance of lower-cost oil for the long-term health of the U.S. economy. A focus on preventing increases in oil prices undercuts the achievement of another major policy goal, the reduction in U.S. consumption of fossil fuels and the U.S. government's commitment to reduce U.S. emissions of carbon dioxide and other greenhouse gases.

Energy Poor. The U.S. government has somewhat more economic leverage with the energy poor than with the energy rich. U.S. foreign assistance to Egypt, Jordan, and Morocco has been substantial. These countries have fewer resources to fall back on and thus rely more heavily on lending from the World Bank and, potentially, the IMF, than do the energy-rich countries.

The U.S. government should continue to push both bilaterally and through its role as a board member of both the World Bank and the IMF for the adoption of policies that have been successful in the Middle East and elsewhere in the developing world: reductions in barriers to trade in goods and services, including financial markets; creating more-favorable conditions for foreign direct investment; and increasing national governments' transparency so as to reduce corruption. The United States should work closely with these international financial institutions to encourage these countries to better target subsidies and reduce costs and hurdles that the private sector faces. The United States also has some bilateral policy instruments at its disposal. Free-trade agreements with Jordan and other Arab countries have not only fostered gains from trade; they have also served to reduce barriers to entry and improve the local business climate. The U.S. government should negotiate and sign more free-trade agreements with friendly countries in the region.

References

"6 Alāf Dullar li Kul Aris fī Suria [$6,000 for Every Groom in Syria]," *Al-Arabiya.net*, June 28, 2004.

Abdallah, Khanjar Wabel, Philippe Callier, Taline Koranchelian, and Michael Lazare, *Algeria: Selected Issues and Statistical Appendix*, Washington, D.C.: International Monetary Fund, country report 03.69, February 7, 2003.

Abdel-Razek, Sherine, "The Cost of Budgeting," *al-Ahram Weekly*, June 19, 2008.

Abdulla, Rasha A., "Taking the E-Train: The Development of the Internet in Egypt," *Global Media and Communication*, Vol. 1, No. 2, August 2005, pp. 149–165.

Abi-Esber, Fouad Daoud, *The Rise and Fall of Christian Minorities in Lebanon*, Sydney: Academic Research, 2005.

Abraham, Salim, "Iraqi Christians Flee to Syria Because of Pressure from Muslim Extremists," Associated Press, August 2004.

Abrahamian, Ervand, *Iran Between Two Revolutions*, Princeton, N.J.: Princeton University Press, 1982. As of October 1, 2010:
http://hdl.handle.net/2027/heb.00853

Agénor, P.-R., M. K. Nabli, T. Yousef, and H. T. Jensen, *Labor Market Reforms, Growth, and Unemployment in Labor-Exporting Countries in the Middle East and North Africa*, World Bank: Policy Research Working Paper 3328, June 2004.

Ajami, Fouad, "What the Muslim World Is Watching," *New York Times Magazine*, November 18, 2001. As of October 1, 2010:
http://www.nytimes.com/2001/11/18/magazine/what-the-muslim-world-is-watching.html

Al-Awadi, Hesham, "Mubarak and the Islamists: Why Did the 'Honeymoon' End?" *Middle East Journal*, Vol. 59, No. 1, Winter 2005, pp. 62–80.

Al-Habib, Abdul Rahman, "The Faultlines in Arab Media Analysis," *Jane's Islamic Affairs Analyst*, July 28, 2006a.

———, "Understanding Arab Media Analysis," *Jane's Islamic Affairs Analyst*, August 2, 2006b.

Ali, Ali Abdel Gadir, *Building Human Capital for Economic Development in the Arab Countries*, Cairo, Egypt: Egyptian Center for Economic Studies, working paper 76, December 2002. As of October 1, 2010:
http://www.eces.org.eg/Publications/View_Pub.asp?p_id=10&p_detail_id=137#mytop

Al-Munajjed, Mona, *Women in Saudi Arabia Today*, New York: St. Martin's Press, 1997.

"Al-Qaeda Online: Understanding Jihadist Internet Infrastructure," *Jane's Intelligence Review*, January 1, 2006.

"al-Saudia: 76 percent min al- Āilāt Jāmiīāt wa Ghālabīyat al-Ālīn min al-amlat al-Thanawiyya [Saudi Arabia: 76 Percent of Unemployed Women Are University Graduates and the Majority of Unemployed Males Are from the Ranks of High School Graduates]," *Asharq al-Awsat*, September 15, 2008.

Al-Sayyid, Mustapha Kamel, "The Concept of Civil Society and the Arab World," in Rex Brynen, Bahgat Korany, and Paul Noble, eds., *Political Liberalization and Democratization in the Arab World*, Vol. I: *Theoretical Perspectives*, Boulder, Colo.: Lynne Rienner Publishers, 1995, pp. 131–148.

Alterman, Jon B., *New Media, New Politics? From Satellite Television to the Internet in the Arab World*, Washington, D.C.: Washington Institute for Near East Policy, 1998.

Amin, Hussein, "Nilesat: Current Challenges and Future Trends," *Transnational Broadcasting Studies*, Vol. 12, Spring–Summer 2004. As of October 1, 2010:
http://www.tbsjournal.com/amin.htm

Anderson, Lisa, "Democracy in the Arab World: A Critique of the Political Culture Approach," in Rex Brynen, Bahgat Korany, and Paul Noble, eds., *Political Liberalization and Democratization in the Arab World*, Vol. I: *Theoretical Perspectives*, Boulder, Colo.: Lynne Rienner Publishers, 1995, pp. 77–92.

Ansary, Abdou Filali, "The Challenge of Secularization," in Larry Jay Diamond, Marc F. Plattner, and Daniel Brumberg, eds., *Islam and Democracy in the Middle East*, Baltimore and London: Johns Hopkins University Press, 2003, pp. 232–236.

Baaklini, Abdo I., Guilain Denoeux, and Robert Springborg, *Legislative Politics in the Arab World: The Resurgence of Democratic Institutions*, Boulder, Colo.: Lynne Rienner Publishers, 1999.

Baki, Roula, "Gender-Segregated Education in Saudi Arabia: Its Impact on Social Norms [and] the Saudi Labor Market," *Education Policy Analysis Archives*, Vol. 12, No. 28, June 17, 2004. As of October 1, 2010:
http://epaa.asu.edu/ojs/article/view/183

Baqi, Mahmoud M. Abdul, and Nansen G. Saleri, "Fifty-Year Crude Oil Supply Scenarios: Saudi Aramco's Perspective," Washington, D.C.: Center for Strategic and International Studies, February 24, 2004. As of October 1, 2010:
http://csis.org/files/media/csis/events/040224_baqiandsaleri.pdf

Baram, Amatzia, *Who Are the Insurgents? Sunni Arab Rebels in Iraq*, Washington, D.C.: U.S. Institute of Peace, special report 134, April 2005. As of October 2, 2010:
http://purl.access.gpo.gov/GPO/LPS60512

Bedjaoui, Ahmed, "Arab and European Satellites over the Maghrib," *Transnational Broadcasting Studies*, Vol. 12, Spring–Summer 2004. As of October 1, 2010:
http://www.tbsjournal.com/maghreb.htm

Benard, Cheryl, *Civil Democratic Islam: Partners, Resources, and Strategies*, Santa Monica, Calif.: RAND Corporation, MR-1716-CMEPP, 2004. As of October 1, 2010:
http://www.rand.org/pubs/monograph_reports/MR1716.html

Benjamin, Daniel, and Steven Simon, *The Age of Sacred Terror*, New York: Random House, 2002.

Benmelech, Efraim, and Claude Berrebi, "Human Capital and the Productivity of Suicide Bombers," *Journal of Economic Perspectives*, Vol. 21, No. 3, Summer 2007, pp. 223–238.

Bensahel, Nora, "Political Reform in the Middle East," in Nora Bensahel and Daniel L. Byman, eds., *The Future Security Environment in the Middle East: Conflict, Stability, and Political Change*, Santa Monica, Calif.: RAND Corporation, MR-1640-AF, 2004, pp. 15–56. As of October 1, 2010:
http://www.rand.org/pubs/monograph_reports/MR1640.html

Berman, Eli, "Sect, Subsidy, and Sacrifice: An Economist's View of Ultra-Orthodox Jews," *Quarterly Journal of Economics*, Vol. 115, No. 3, August 2000, pp. 905–953.

Bernstein, Mark, David G. Groves, and Amber Moreen, "Water," in RAND Palestinian State Study Team, *Building a Successful Palestinian State*, Santa Monica, Calif.: RAND Corporation, MG-146-1-DCR, 2007, pp. 163–221. As of October 14, 2010:
http://www.rand.org/pubs/monographs/MG146-1.html

Berrebi, Claude, "Evidence About the Link Between Education, Poverty and Terrorism Among Palestinians," *Peace Economics, Peace Science and Public Policy*, Vol. 13, No. 1, Art. 2, 2007. As of October 1, 2010:
http://www.bepress.com/peps/vol13/iss1/2/

Bilingsley, Dodge, "War on Film: The Often Fraught Relationship Between Military and Media," *Jane's Intelligence Review*, July 1, 2007.

Black, Andrew, and Shane Drennan, "Jihad Online: The Changing Role of the Internet," *Jane's Intelligence Review*, August 1, 2007.

Blanchard, Christopher M., *Al Qaeda: Statements and Evolving Ideology*, Washington, D.C.: Congressional Research Service, report for Congress RL32759, July 9, 2007. As of October 1, 2010:
http://www.fas.org/sgp/crs/terror/RL32759.pdf

Blandford, Nicholas, "Chaos Returns to Troubled Lebanon," *Jane's Defence Weekly*, Vol. 44, No. 22, May 30, 2007.

Blass, Asher, and Richard S. Grossman, "Assessing Damages: The 1983 Israeli Bank Shares Crisis," *Contemporary Economic Policy*, Vol. 19, No. 1, January 2001, pp. 49–58.

Blavy, Rodolphe, *Trade in the Mashreq: An Empirical Examination*, Washington, D.C.: International Monetary Fund, Middle Eastern Department, working paper 01/163, October 1, 2001. As of October 1, 2010:
http://www.imf.org/external/pubs/cat/longres.cfm?sk=15426.0

Bloom, Mia M., "Palestinian Suicide Bombing: Public Support, Market Share, and Outbidding," *Political Science Quarterly*, Vol. 119, No. 1, Spring 2004, pp. 61–88.

Bonanate, Luigi, "Some Unanticipated Consequences of Terrorism," *Journal of Peace Research*, Vol. 16, No. 3, September 1979, pp. 197–211.

Boyd, Douglas, "Saudi Arabia's International Media Strategy: Influence through Multinational Ownership," in Kai Hafez, ed., *Mass Media, Politics, and Society in the Middle East*, Cresskill, N.J.: Hampton Press, 2001, pp. 43–60.

BP Statistical Review of World Energy, June 2008, using data provided by the Energy Information Administration, U.S. Department of Energy, on January 8, 2008.

Brownlee, Jason M., "The Decline of Pluralism in Mubarek's Egypt," in Larry Jay Diamond, Marc F. Plattner, and Daniel Brumberg, eds., *Islam and Democracy in the Middle East*, Baltimore, Md.: Johns Hopkins University Press, 2003, pp. 48–57.

———, *Ruling Parties and Durable Authoritarianism*, Stanford, Calif.: Center on Democracy, Development, and the Rule of Law, Freeman Spogli Institute for International Studies, October 28, 2004. As of October 1, 2010:
http://cddrl.stanford.edu/publications/ruling_parties_and_durable_authoritarianism/

Bruce, James, "Arab Veterans of the Afghan War," *Jane's Intelligence Review*, Vol. 7, No. 4, April 1995.

Brumberg, Daniel, "Democratization in the Arab World? The Trap of Liberalized Autocracy," *Journal of Democracy*, Vol. 13, No. 4, October 2002, pp. 56–68.

———, "The Trap of Liberalizing Autocracies," in Larry Jay Diamond, Marc F. Plattner, and Daniel Brumberg, eds., *Islam and Democracy in the Middle East*, Baltimore, Md.: Johns Hopkins University Press, 2003a, pp. 35–47.

———, *Liberalization Versus Democracy: Understanding Arab Political Reform*, Washington, D.C.: Carnegie Endowment for International Peace, working paper 37, May 2003b.

Burton, Fred, and Scott Stewart, "The July 4 Al-Zawahiri Video: Protesting Too Much," *Stratfor*, July 11, 2007.

Byman, Daniel, Peter Chalk, Bruce Hoffman, William Rosenau, and David Brannan, *Trends in Outside Support for Insurgent Movements*, Santa Monica, Calif.: RAND Corporation, MR-1405-OTI, 2001. As of October 1, 2010:
http://www.rand.org/pubs/monograph_reports/MR1405.html

Cardenas, Sonia, and Andrew Flibbert, "National Human Rights Institutions in the Middle East," *Middle East Journal*, Vol. 59, No. 3, Summer 2005, pp. 411–436.

Central Intelligence Agency, *The World Factbook*, Washington, D.C., updated weekly.

———, "Egypt," *World Factbook*, last updated January 13, 2011. As of February 7, 2011:
https://www.cia.gov/library/publications/the-world-factbook/geos/eg.html

Central Organization for Statistics and Information Technology, *Unemployment Survey 2006*.

Chamlou, Nadereh, "Gender and Development in the Middle East and North Africa," World Bank, briefing prepared for the Woodrow Wilson Center, January 30, 2004.

Chaudhry, Kiren Aziz, *The Price of Wealth: Economies and Institutions in the Middle East*, Ithaca, N.Y.: Cornell University Press, 1997.

CIA—*See* Central Intelligence Agency.

Collier, Paul, *Breaking the Conflict Trap: Civil War and Development Policy*, Washington, D.C.: World Bank, 2003.

Cook, David, "The Recovery of Radical Islam in the Wake of the Defeat of the Taliban," *Terrorism and Political Violence*, Vol. 15, No. 1, Spring 2003, pp. 31–56.

Cordesman, Anthony H., *After the Storm: The Changing Military Balance in the Middle East*, Boulder, Colo.: Westview Press, 1993.

Coulson, Andrew, "Education and Indoctrination in the Muslim World: Is There a Problem? What Can We Do About It?" *Policy Analysis*, No. 511, March 11, 2004. As of October 1, 2010:
http://www.cato.org/pubs/pas/pa511.pdf

Cronin, Audrey Kurth, *Al Qaeda After the Iraq Conflict*, Washington, D.C.: Congressional Research Service, RS21529, 2003. As of October 1, 2010:
http://purl.access.gpo.gov/GPO/LPS38560

Crumpton, Henry, "Al-Qaeda Crippled but Resilient," interview by Robert McMahon, Council on Foreign Relations, August 21, 2006. As of October 1, 2010:
http://www.cfr.org/publication/11318/alqaeda_crippled_but_resilient.html

Das Gupta, Dipak, Jennifer Keller, and T. G. Srinivasan, *Reform and Elusive Growth in the Middle East: What Has Happened in the 1990s?* Washington, D.C.: World Bank, Human Development Group, Middle East and North Africa Region, working paper 25, June 2002.

DeBartolo, David M., "Jordan: Attention Turns to Electoral Law," *Arab Reform Bulletin*, Vol. 5, No. 3, April 2, 2007. As of October 1, 2010:
http://www.carnegieendowment.org/arb/?fa=show&article=21266

Denoeux, Guilain, "The Forgotten Swamp: Navigating Political Islam," *Middle East Policy*, Vol. 9, No. 2, June 2002, pp. 56–81.

Diamond, Larry, *Political Culture and Democracy in Developing Countries*, Boulder, Colo.: L. Rienner Publishers, 1993.

———, "Introduction: In Search of Consolidation," in Larry Diamond, Marc F. Plattner, Yun-han Chu, and Hung-mao Tien, eds., *Consolidating Third Wave Democracies: Themes and Perspectives*, Baltimore, Md.: Johns Hopkins University Press, 1997, pp. xiii–xlvii.

Diamond, Larry Jay, Marc F. Plattner, and Daniel Brumberg, eds., *Islam and Democracy in the Middle East*, Baltimore, Md.: Johns Hopkins University Press, 2003.

Diwan, Ishac, and Radwan `Ali Sha`ban, *Development Under Adversity: The Palestinian Economy in Transition*, Washington, D.C.: World Bank, March 1999. As of October 2, 2010:
http://www.worldbank.icebox.ingenta.com/content/wb/411

Djankov, Simeon, Tatiana Nenova, Caralee McLiesh, and Andrei Shleifer, "Who Owns the Media?" *Journal of Law and Economics*, Vol. 46, No. 2, October 2003, pp. 341–381.

Dobriansky, Paula J., Under Secretary for Global Affairs, and Michael Kozak, Acting Assistant Secretary for Democracy Human Rights and Labor, U.S. Department of State, "On-the-Record Briefing on the Release of the 2004 Annual Report on Human Rights," Washington, D.C., February 28, 2005. As of October 1, 2010:
http://2001-2009.state.gov/g/drl/rls/spbr/42805.htm

Dollar, David, Raymond Fisman, and Roberta Gatti, *Are Women Really the "Fairer" Sex? Corruption and Women in Government*, Washington, D.C.: World Bank, Development Research Group, Poverty Reduction and Economic Management Network, policy research report on gender and development working paper 4, October 1999.

Doran, Michael Scott, "Somebody Else's Civil War," *Foreign Affairs*, January–February 2002.

Economic Commission for Africa, "Egypt," *National Information and Communication Infrastructure (NICI) Policies and Plans (e-strategies)*, undated web page. As of October 14, 2010:
http://www.uneca.org/AISI/nici/Egypt/egypt.htm

Ehteshami, Anoushiravan, "Reform from Above: The Politics of Participation in the Oil Monarchies," *International Affairs*, Vol. 79, No. 1, January 2003, pp. 53–75.

EIA—*See* Energy Information Administration.

El-Ghobashy, Mona, "Egypt Looks Ahead to Portentous Year," *Middle East Report Online*, February 2, 2005. As of October 1, 2010:
http://www.merip.org/mero/mero020205.html

El Qorchi, Mohammed, Samuel Munzele Maimbo, and John F. Wilson, *Informal Funds Transfer Systems: An Analysis of the Informal Hawala System*, Washington, D.C.: International Monetary Fund occasional paper 222, 2003.

Energy Information Administration, "International Energy Statistics," undated web page. As of October 18, 2010:
http://tonto.eia.doe.gov/cfapps/ipdbproject/IEDIndex3.cfm?tid=5&pid=57&aid=6

———, *International Energy Outlook 2004*, DOE/EIA-0484(2004), April 2004. As of October 18, 2010:
http://www.eia.doe.gov/oiaf/archive/ieo04/index.html

———, *Annual Energy Outlook 2007 with Projections to 2030*, DOE/EIA-0383(2007), February 2007a. As of October 1, 2010:
http://www.eia.doe.gov/oiaf/archive/aeo07/index.html

———, *International Energy Outlook 2007*, DOE/EIA-0484(2007), May 2007b. As of October 1, 2010:
http://www.eia.doe.gov/oiaf/archive/ieo07/index.html

———, "World Production of Crude Oil, NGPL, and Other Liquids, and Refinery Processing Gain, Most Recent Annual Estimates, 1980–2007," December 19, 2008. As of October 1, 2010:
http://www.eia.doe.gov/emeu/international/RecentTotalOilSupplyBarrelsperDay.xls

———, *Annual Energy Outlook 2009*, DOE/EIA-0383(2009), March 2009a. As of October 1, 2010:
http://www.eia.doe.gov/oiaf/archive/aeo09/index.html

———, *International Energy Outlook 2009*, DOE/EIA-0484(2009), May 27, 2009b. As of October 1, 2010:
http://www.eia.doe.gov/oiaf/archive/ieo09/index.html

Esposito, John L., *Islam: The Straight Path*, Oxford: Oxford University Press, 1988.

Fagen, Patricia Weiss, *Iraqi Refugees: Seeking Stability in Syria and Jordan*, Doha: Institute for the Study of International Migration, Center for International and Regional Studies, 2007.

Fair, C. Christine, Keith Crane, Christopher S. Chivvis, Samir Puri, and Michael Spirtas, *Pakistan: Can the United States Secure an Insecure State?* Santa Monica, Calif.: RAND Corporation, MG-910-AF, 2010. As of February 7, 2011:
http://www.rand.org/pubs/monographs/MG910.html

Fandy, Mamoun, "CyberResistance: Saudi Opposition Between Globalization and Localization," *Comparative Studies in Society and History*, Vol. 41, No. 1, January 1999, pp. 124–147.

———, "Information Technology, Trust, and Social Change in the Arab World," *Middle East Journal*, Vol. 54, No. 3, Summer 2000, pp. 378–394.

———, *Arab Media: Tools of the Governments, Tools for the People?* Washington, D.C.: U.S. Institute of Peace, Virtual Diplomacy Series 18, August 2005. As of October 1, 2010:
http://purl.access.gpo.gov/GPO/LPS68385

Fargues, Philippe, "The Arab Christians of the Middle East: A Demographic Perspective," in Andrea Pacini, ed., *Christian Communities in the Arab Middle East: The Challenge of the Future*, Oxford: Clarendon Press, 1998, pp. 48–66.

———, "Protracted National Conflict and Fertility Change: Palestinians and Israelis in the Twentieth Century," *Population and Development Review*, Vol. 26, No. 3, September 2000, pp. 441–482.

Fasano, Ugo, and Zubair Iqbal, "Common Currency," *Finance and Development*, Vol. 39, No. 4, December 2002. As of October 1, 2010:
http://www.imf.org/external/pubs/ft/fandd/2002/12/fasano.htm

Fedderke, Johannes, and Robert Klitgaard, "Economic Growth and Social Indicators: An Exploratory Analysis," *Economic Development and Cultural Change*, Vol. 46, No. 3, April 1998, pp. 455–489.

Ficklin, Lisa, "The Groupes Islamistes Armées (GIA)," Islamic Institute for Human Rights, date unknown.

Fuller, Graham, "Islamists and Democracy," in Thomas Carothers and Marina Ottoway, ed., *Uncharted Journey: Promoting Democracy in the Middle East*, Washington, D.C.: Carnegie Endowment for International Peace, Brookings Institution Press, 2005, pp. 37–56.

Fuller, Graham E., *The Youth Factor: The New Demographics of the Middle East and the Implications for U.S. Policy*, Washington, D.C.: Saban Center for Middle East Policy at the Brookings Institution, analysis paper 3, June 2003. As of October 1, 2010:
http://www.brookings.edu/papers/2003/06middleeast_fuller.aspx

Garon, Lise, "The Press and Democratic Transition in Arab Societies: The Algerian Case," in Rex Brynen, Bahgat Korany, and Paul Noble, eds., *Political Liberalization and Democratization in the Arab World*, Vol. 1, Boulder, Colo.: Lynne Reinner, 1995, pp. 149–166.

Gause, F. Gregory III, *Oil Monarchies: Domestic and Security Challenges in the Arab Gulf States*, New York: Council on Foreign Relations, 1993.

Gentskow, Matthew A., and Jesse M. Shapiro, "Media, Education, and Anti-Americanism in the Muslim World," *Journal of Economic Perspectives*, Vol. 18, No. 3, Summer 2004, pp. 117–133.

Gerth, Jeff, "Forecast of Rising Oil Demand Challenges Tired Saudi Fields," *New York Times*, February 24, 2004. As of October 18, 2010:
http://www.nytimes.com/2004/02/24/business/forecast-of-rising-oil-demand-challenges-tired-saudi-fields.html

Ghareeb, Edmund, "New Media and the Information Revolution in the Arab World: An Assessment," *Middle East Journal*, Vol. 54, No. 3, Summer 2000, pp. 395–418.

Gokcekus, Omer and Ranjana Mukherjee, "Gender and Corruption in the Public Sector," World Bank, July 2002.

Gregorian, Vartan, *The Emergence of Modern Afghanistan: Politics of Reform and Modernization, 1880–1946*, Stanford, Calif.: Stanford University Press, 1969.

"Guide: Christians in the Middle East," *BBC News*, December 15, 2005. As of October 14, 2010:
http://news.bbc.co.uk/2/hi/middle_east/4499668.stm

Gurr, Ted Robert, ed., *Minorities at Risk: A Global View of Ethnopolitical Conflicts*, Washington, D.C.: U.S. Institute of Peace, 1993.

Gürsoy, Akile, "Child Mortality and the Changing Discourse on Childhood in Turkey," in Elizabeth Warnock Fernea, ed., *Children in the Muslim Middle East*, Austin, Texas: University of Texas Press, 1995, pp. 199–222.

Hafez, Kai, ed., *Mass Media, Politics, and Society in the Middle East*, Cresskill, N.J.: Hampton Press, 2001.

Haqqani, Husain, "Islam's Medieval Outposts," *Foreign Policy*, November 1, 2002.

Hardy, Roger, "Migrants Demand Labour Rights in Gulf," *BBC News*, February 27, 2008. As of October 19, 2010:
http://news.bbc.co.uk/2/hi/middle_east/7266610.stm

Harff, Barbara, "Minorities, Rebellion, and Repression in North Africa and the Middle East," in Ted Robert Gurr, ed., *Minorities at Risk: A Global View of Ethnopolitical Conflicts*, Washington, D.C.: U.S. Institute of Peace, 1993.

Harik, Judith Palmer, "Between Islam and the System: Sources and Implications of Popular Support for Lebanon's Hizballah," *Journal of Conflict Resolution*, Vol. 40, No. 1, March 1996, pp. 41–67.

Harmon, Christopher, "Five Strategies of Terrorism," *Small Wars and Insurgencies*, Vol. 12, No. 3, Autumn 2001, pp. 39–66.

Harris, William W., *Faces of Lebanon: Sects, Wars, and Global Extensions*, Princeton, N.J.: Markus Wiener Publishers, 1997.

Hassan, Najla, "Arāqīl Thaqāfiyya wa Bīiyya amam Tanīm al-Usra fī al-Yaman [Cultural and Environmental Impediments Facing Family Planning in Yemen]," *al-Hayat*, August 5, 2008.

Hatina, Meir, *Islam and Salvation in Palestine: The Islamic Jihad Movement*, Tel Aviv: Moshe Dayan Center for Middle Eastern and African Studies, Tel Aviv University, 2001.

Hawthorne, Amy, "Is Civil Society the Answer?" in Thomas Carothers and Marina Ottoway, eds., *Uncharted Journey: Promoting Democracy in the Middle East*, Washington, D.C.: Carnegie Endowment for International Peace, Brookings Institution Press, 2005, pp. 81–114.

Haykel, Bernard, "Radical Salafism: Osama's Ideology," *Dawn*, December 8, 2001.

Hefner, Robert, "Civic Pluralism Denied? The New Media and Jihadi Violence in Indonesia," in Dale F. Eickelman and Jon W. Anderson, eds., *New Media in the Muslim World*, Bloomington, Ind.: Indiana University Press, 2003, pp. 158–179.

Herb, Michael, "Princes and Parliaments in the Arab World," *Middle East Journal*, Vol. 58, No. 3, July 2004, pp. 367–384.

Herbst, Jeffrey, "Prospects for Elite-Driven Democracy in South Africa," *Political Science Quarterly*, Vol. 112, No. 4, Winter 1997–1998, pp. 595–615.

Hess, Stephen, *Through Their Eyes: Foreign Correspondents in the United States*, Washington, D.C.: Brookings Institution Press, 2005.

Hoffman, Bruce, *The Use of the Internet by Islamic Extremists*, Santa Monica, Calif.: RAND Corporation, CT-262-1, 2006. As of October 1, 2010:
http://www.rand.org/pubs/testimonies/CT262-1.html

———, "The Global Terrorist Threat: Is Al-Qaeda on the Run or on the March?" *Middle East Policy*, Vol. 14, No. 2, June 2007, pp. 44–58.

Hudson, Michael C., "The Political Culture Approach to Arab Democratization: The Case for Bringing It Back In, Carefully," in Rex Brynen, Bahgat Korany, and Paul Noble, eds., *Political Liberalization and Democratization in the Arab World*, Vol. I: *Theoretical Perspectives*, Boulder, Colo.: Lynne Rienner Publishers, 1995, pp. 61–76.

Huntington, Samuel P., *The Clash of Civilizations and the Remaking of World Order*, New York: Simon and Schuster, 1996.

Huntington, Samuel P., and Lawrence E. Harrison, eds., *Culture Matters: How Values Shape Human Progress*, New York: Basic Books, 2000.

Ibrahim, Anwar, "Universal Values and Muslim Democracies," *Journal of Democracy*, Vol. 17, No. 3, July 2006, pp. 5–12.

Ibrahim, Saad Eddin, "Anatomy of Egypt's Islamic Groups: Methodological Note and Preliminary Findings," *International Journal of Middle East Studies*, Vol. 12, No. 4, December 1980, pp. 423–453.

———, "Toward Muslim Democracies," *Journal of Democracy*, Vol. 18, No. 2, April 2007, pp. 5–13.

ILO—*See* International Labour Organization.

IMF—*See* International Monetary Fund.

International Crisis Group, *Iran in Iraq: How Much Influence?* Amman, Middle East report 38, March 21, 2005.

———, *The Next Iraqi War? Sectarian and Civil Conflict*, Baghdad, Middle East report 52, February 27, 2006a.

———, *Iraq's Muqtada Al-Sadr: Spoiler or Stabiliser*, Amman, Middle East report 55, July 11, 2006b.

———, *Iraq and the Kurds: Resolving the Kirkuk Crisis*, Middle East Report 64, April 19, 2007. As of February 8, 2011:
http://www.rcusa.org/uploads/pdfs/ICG,%20Iraq%20and%20the%20Kurds,%204-18-07.pdf

International Energy Agency, *Oil Market Report*, Paris, January 16, 2008. As of October 1, 2010:
http://omrpublic.iea.org/omrarchive/16jan08full.pdf

International Labour Organization, *Key Indicators of the Labour Market, 2001–2002*, New York: Routledge, 2002.

International Monetary Fund, "Saudi Arabia," *International Financial Statistics*, undated.

———, *Tunisia: 2003 Article IV Consultation—Staff Report, Staff Supplement, Public Information Notice on the Executive Board Discussion and Statement by the Executive Director for Tunisia*, country report 03/259, 2003a.

———, *The Socialist People's Libyan Arab Jamahiriya: 2003 Article IV Consultation—Staff Report, Staff Statement, Public Information Notice on the Executive Board Discussion*, country report 03/327, October 2003b. As of October 1, 2010:
http://www.imf.org/external/pubs/cat/longres.cfm?sk=16952.0

———, "Egypt," *International Financial Statistics*, Washington, D.C.: April 2004a.

———, *Israel: 2003 Article IV Consultation—Staff Report, Staff Statement, and Public Information Notice on the Executive Board Discussion*, country report 2004-158, June 2004b. As of October 1, 2010:
http://www.imf.org/external/pubs/ft/scr/2004/cr04158.pdf

———, *Morocco: 2004 Article IV Consultation—Staff Report, Public Information Notice on the Executive Board Discussion, and Statement by the Executive Director for Morocco*, Washington, D.C., June 2004c.

———, "IMF Concludes 2004 Article IV Consultation with the Arab Republic of Egypt," public information notice 04/69, July 12, 2004d. As of October 1, 2010:
http://www.imf.org/external/np/sec/pn/2004/pn0469.htm

———, *Morocco: 2007 Article IV Consultation—Staff Report, Staff Statement, Public Information Notice on the Executive Board Discussion, and Statement by the Executive Director for Morocco*, Washington, D.C., country report 07/323, September 2007a. As of October 19, 2010:
http://www.imf.org/external/pubs/cat/longres.cfm?sk=21346.0

———, *Arab Republic of Egypt: 2007 Article IV Consultation—Staff Report, Staff Statement, Public Information Notice on the Executive Board Discussion, and Statement by the Executive Director for the Arab Republic of Egypt*, Washington, D.C., country report 07/380, December 2007b. As of October 1, 2010:
http://www.imf.org/external/pubs/cat/longres.cfm?sk=21507.0

———, "International Financial Statistics: Commodity Prices," global database, 1970–2008.

———, *World Economic Outlook (WEO): Crisis and Recovery*, Washington, D.C., April 2009. As of October 19, 2010:
http://www.imf.org/external/pubs/ft/weo/2009/01/

"Iran's Second Revolution?" *Economist*, July 19, 1999.

Ismail, Salwa, "Democracy in Contemporary Arab Intellectual Discourse," in Rex Brynen, Bahgat Korany, and Paul Noble, eds., *Political Liberalization and Democratization in the Arab World*, Vol. I: *Theoretical Perspectives*, Boulder, Colo.: Lynne Rienner Publishers, 1995, pp. 93–112.

Israeli Central Bureau of Statistics, *Projections of Israel's Population Until 2020*, c. 1997. As of October 14, 2010:
http://www.cbs.gov.il/mifkad/popul00_00_e.htm

Johnson, Mark, "Libyan Arab Jamahiriya," *New Internationalist*, No. 177, November 1987. As of February 7, 2011:
http://www.newint.org/features/1987/11/05/profile/

Jones, Jeremy, and Nicholas Ridout, "Democratic Development in Oman," *Middle East Journal*, Vol. 59, No. 3, Summer 2005, pp. 376–392.

Kakel, Kamaran, "Who Are the Kurds?" undated web page. As of October 14, 2010:
http://www.cool.mb.ca/~kakel/kurds.html

Kaplan, Eben, "Terrorism's Net War," analysis brief, New York: Council on Foreign Relations, March 2, 2006a.

———, "Al-Qaeda's Media Campaign," New York: Council on Foreign Relations, May 12, 2006b. As of October 1, 2010:
http://www.cfr.org/publication/10678/alqaedas_media_campaign.html

———, "Terrorists and the Internet," backgrounder, New York: Council on Foreign Relations, May 12, 2006c. As of October 1, 2010:
http://www.cfr.org/publication/10005/terrorists_and_the_internet.html

Karl, Terry Lynn, "Dilemmas of Democratization in Latin America," *Comparative Politics*, Vol. 23, No. 1, October 1990, pp. 1–21.

Katzman, Kenneth, *Al Qaeda: Profile and Threat Assessment*, Washington, D.C.: Congressional Research Service, report for Congress RL33038, August 17, 2005.

Kaufmann, Daniel, and Aart Kraay, "Governance and Growth: Causality Which Way? Evidence for the World, in Brief," Washington, D.C.: World Bank, February 2003. As of October 1, 2010:
http://info.worldbank.org/etools/library/view_p.asp?lprogram=5&objectid=18033

Keating, Benjamin, "In the Spotlight: Moroccan Combatant Group (GICM)," Center for Defense Information, May 21, 2004.

Kéchichian, Joseph A., "Democratization in Gulf Monarchies: A New Challenge to the GCC," *Middle East Policy*, Vol. 11, No. 4, December 2004, pp. 37–57.

Khairi, Amina, "al-Tiliviziyūn Laab Dawrān Kabīrān . . . al-Tamwīl al-Ajanabī Yansaib min Tanīm al-Nasl fi Misr [The Television Played a Major Role: Foreign Funding Is Falling Back in Family Planning in Egypt]," *al-Hayat*, October 17, 2006.

Kjeilen, Tore, "Berbers," *LookLex Encyclopaedia*, undated web page. As of October 14, 2010:
http://lexicorient.com/e.o/berbers.htm

Kramer, Karen, "Arab Political Pacts: An Unlikely Scenario," *Journal of Democracy*, Vol. 17, No. 4, October 2006, pp. 160–165.

Lambsdorff, Johann Graf, "Corruption Perceptions Index 2006," Transparency International, November 6, 2006. As of October 1, 2010:
http://www.transparency.org/policy_research/surveys_indices/cpi/2006

———, "Corruption Perceptions Index 2007," Transparency International, September 26, 2007. As of October 2, 2010:
http://www.transparency.org/policy_research/surveys_indices/cpi/2007

———, "Corruption Perceptions Index 2008," Transparency International, September 22, 2008. As of October 18, 2010:
http://www.transparency.org/policy_research/surveys_indices/cpi/2008

Landes, David S., *The Wealth and Poverty of Nations: Why Some Are So Rich and Some So Poor*, New York: W. W. Norton, 1998.

Larrabee, F. Stephen, *Troubled Partnership: U.S.-Turkish Relations in an Era of Global Geopolitical Change*, Santa Monica, Calif.: RAND Corporation, MG-899-AF, 2010. As of February 7, 2011:
http://www.rand.org/pubs/monographs/MG899.html

Laskier, Michael M., "A Difficult Inheritance: Moroccan Society Under King Muhammad VI," *Middle East Review of International Affairs*, Vol. 7, No. 3, September 2003. As of October 1, 2010:
http://www.muslimpersonallaw.co.za/A%20Difficult%20Inheritance1.pdf

Lazare, Michel, Philippe Callier, Khanjar Wabel Abdallah, and Taline Koranchelian, *Algeria: Selected Issues and Statistical Appendix*, International Monetary Fund, January 29, 2003. As of January 24, 2011:
http://www.imf.org/external/pubs/cat/longres.cfm?sk=16414.0

Levine, Mark, "National Elections in the Middle East and Arab World Since 1980," *Middle East Report*, Winter 1998.

Lewis, Bernard, "The West and the Middle East," *Foreign Affairs*, January–February 1997.

———, *What Went Wrong? The Clash Between Islam and Modernity in the Middle East*, New York: Perennial, 2002.

Maluf, Ramez, "Review Article: Al Jazeera: The Enfant Terrible of Arab Media," *European Journal of Communication*, Vol. 20, No. 4, 2005, pp. 531–537. As of October 1, 2010:
http://ejc.sagepub.com/content/20/4/531.full.pdf+html

Martin, Vanessa, *Islam and Modernism: The Iranian Revolution of 1906*, Syracuse, N.Y.: Syracuse University Press, 1989.

McCarthy, Kevin F., *The Palestine Refugee Issue: One Perspective*, Santa Monica, Calif.: RAND Corporation, DRU-1358-GMSEC, 1996. As of January 24, 2011:
http://www.rand.org/pubs/drafts/DRU1358.html

McCarthy, Kevin F., and Brian Nichiporuk, "Demography," in RAND Palestinian State Study Team, *Building a Successful Palestinian State*, Santa Monica, Calif.: RAND Corporation, MG-146-1-DCR, 2004, pp. 73–106. As of October 1, 2010:
http://www.rand.org/pubs/monographs/MG146-1.html

Mehlis, Detlev, *Report of the International Independent Investigation Commission Established Pursuant to Security Council Resolution 1595 (2005)*, Beirut, October 19, 2005. As of October 2, 2010:
http://media.washingtonpost.com/wp-srv/world/pdfs/mehlisReport.pdf

Miles, Hugh, *Al-Jazeera: The Inside Story of the Arab News Channel That Is Challenging the West*, New York: Grove Press, 2005.

Milton-Edwards, Beverly, "Façade Democracy and Jordan," *British Journal of Middle Eastern Studies*, Vol. 20, No. 2, 1993, pp. 191–203.

Moreland, Scott, *Egypt's Population Program: Assessing 25 Years of Family Planning*, Washington, D.C.: U.S. Agency for International Development, March 2006. As of October 14, 2010:
http://www.policyproject.com/pubs/countryreports/Egypt%2025%20yr%20retro%20Final.pdf

Mouawad, Ray J., "Syria and Iraq—Repression: Disappearing Christians of the Middle East," *Middle East Quarterly*, Vol. VIII, No. 1, Winter 2001, pp. 51–50. As of October 14, 2010:
http://www.meforum.org/17/syria-and-iraq-repression

Murasilu al-Jazira [Al Jazeera's correspondents], "al-Shabāb al-Suri wa āhirat al-Azūf an al-Zawāj [Syrian Youth and the Aversion to Marriage Phenomenon]," *Al-Jazeera.net*, October 28, 2006.

Nashashibi, Karim A., *Fiscal Revenues in South Mediterranean Arab Countries: Vulnerabilities and Growth Potential*, Washington, D.C.: International Monetary Fund, working paper 02/67, April 2002. As of October 1, 2010:
http://www.imf.org/external/pubs/cat/longres.cfm?sk=15587.0

Nasrallah, al-Sayyid Hassan, "al-Sīra al-Dhātiya [Autobiography]," *al-Mustaqbal al-Arabi*, September 2006.

National Counterterrorism Center, *2007 Report on Terrorism*, Washington, D.C., April 30, 2008. As of October 14, 2010:
http://www.nctc.gov/witsbanner/docs/2007_report_on_terrorism.pdf

Noland, Marcus, and Howard Pack, *The Arab Economies in a Changing World*, Washington, D.C.: Peterson Institute for International Economics, April 2007.

Norton, Augustus Richard, "Introduction," in Augustus R. Norton, ed., *Civil Society in the Middle East*, Vol. I, Leiden: Brill, 1995, pp. 1–26.

Office of the Director of National Intelligence, National Intelligence Council, *The Terrorist Threat to the U.S. Homeland*, Washington, D.C., July 2007. As of October 1, 2010:
http://purl.access.gpo.gov/GPO/LPS83984

"OPEC Members' Cheating on Quotas Increases," *Bloomberg News*, January 19, 2010. As of February 7, 2011:
http://www.chron.com/disp/story.mpl/business/6825432.html

Organisation for Economic Co-Operation and Development (OECD), *Trends in International Migration: Continuous Reporting System on Migration*, Paris, 2001.

Ottaway, Marina, *Democracy Challenged: The Rise of Semi-Authoritarianism*, Washington, D.C.: Carnegie Endowment for International Peace, 2003.

———, "The Limits of Women's Rights," in Thomas Carothers and Marina Ottoway, eds., *Uncharted Journey: Promoting Democracy in the Middle East*, Washington, D.C.: Carnegie Endowment for International Peace, 2005, pp. 115–130.

Ottaway, Marina S., Jillian Schwedler, Shibley Telhami, and Saad Eddin Ibrahim, "Democracy: Rising Tide or Mirage?" *Middle East Policy*, Vol. 12, No. 2, Summer 2005, pp. 1–27.

Pan, Esther, "Iraq's Media Takes Its First Steps," New York: Council on Foreign Relations, December 13, 2005. As of October 1, 2010:
http://www.cfr.org/publication/9409/iraqs_media_takes_its_first_steps.html

Perl, Raphael, *Trends in Terrorism: 2006*, Washington, D.C.: Congressional Research Service, report for Congress RL33555, March 12, 2007.

Peters, Rudolph, *Islam and Colonialism: The Doctrine of Jihad in Modern History*, The Hague: Mouton, 1979.

Pew Global Attitudes Project, *Views of a Changing World, June 2003: How Global Publics View War in Iraq, Democracy, Islam and Governance, Globalization*, Washington, D.C.: Pew Research Center for the People and the Press, June 3, 2003.

Pew Research Center, *The Great Divide: How Westerners and Muslims View Each Other*, Washington, D.C., June 22, 2006. As of October 2, 2010:
http://pewglobal.org/reports/display.php?ReportID=253

Przeworski, Adam, "Some Problems in the Study of the Transition to Democracy," in Guillermo A. O'Donnell, Philippe C. Schmitter, and Laurence Whitehead, eds., *Transitions from Authoritarian Rule*, Baltimore, Md.: Johns Hopkins University Press, 1986, pp. 47–63.

"Principal Deserts of the World," *infoplease*, 2007. As of October 14, 2010:
http://www.infoplease.com/ipa/A0778851.html

Qaddafi, Muammar, *Green Book*, unauthorized ed., Henry M. Christman, ed., Buffalo, N.Y.: Prometheus Books, 1988.

Rabasa, Angel, *Radical Islam in East Africa*, Santa Monica, Calif.: RAND Corporation, MG-782-AF, 2009. As of February 7, 2011:
http://www.rand.org/pubs/monographs/MG782.html

Rai, Mugdha, and Simon Cottle, "Global Mediations: On the Changing Ecology of Satellite Television News," *Global Media and Communication*, Vol. 3, No. 1, April 2007, pp. 51–78.

Raphaeli, Nimrod, "Ayman Muhammad Rabi' Al-Zawahiri: The Making of an Arch-Terrorist," *Terrorism and Political Violence*, Vol. 14, No. 4, Winter 2002, pp. 1–22.

Ratha, Dilip, "Workers' Remittances: An Important and Stable Source of External Development Finance," *Global Development Finance 2003*, World Bank, 2003, pp. 157–176.

Richards, Alan, and John Waterbury, *A Political Economy of the Middle East*, 2nd ed., Boulder, Colo.: Westview Press, 1996.

Riedel, Bruce, "The Return of the Knights: al-Qaeda and the Fruits of Middle East Disorder," *Survival*, Vol. 49, No. 3, September 2007, pp. 107–120.

Robinson, Glenn E., "Defensive Democratization in Jordan," *International Journal of Middle East Studies*, Vol. 30, No. 3, August 1998, pp. 387–410.

Rosegrant, Mark W., Ximing Cai, and Sarah A. Cline, "The Future of Water and Food in the Middle East and North Africa: Outlook to 2025," Washington, D.C.: International Food Policy Research Institute and Institute and International Water Management Institute, 2002.

Rosenblum, Mort, "Kuwait After the Gulf War: A Painful Insecurity," CBS News, January 14, 2001. As of October 18, 2010:
http://www.cbsnews.com/stories/2001/01/11/gulfwar/main263479.shtml

Ross, Michael Lewin, "Does Oil Hinder Democracy?" *World Politics*, Vol. 53, No. 3, April 2001, pp. 325–361.

Roudi-Fahimi, Farzaneh, "Iran's Family Planning Program: Responding to a Nation's Needs," Washington, D.C.: Population Reference Bureau, June 2002. As of October 14, 2010:
http://www.prb.org/Publications/PolicyBriefs/IransFamilyPlanningProgram.aspx

Roudi-Fahimi, Farzaneh, and Mary Mederios Kent, "Challenges and Opportunities: The Population of the Middle East and North Africa," *Population Bulletin*, Vol. 62, No. 2, June 2007. As of October 14, 2010:
http://www.prb.org/Publications/PopulationBulletins/2007/ChallengesOpportunitiesinMENA.aspx

Rugh, William A., *Arab Mass Media: Newspapers, Radio, and Television in Arab Politics*, Westport, Conn.: Praeger, 2004.

Rustow, Dankwart A., "Transitions to Democracy: Toward a Democratic Model," *Comparative Politics*, Vol. 2, No. 3, April 1970, pp. 337–363.

Ryan, Curtis R., and Jillian Schwedler, "Return to Democratization or New Hybrid Regime? The 2003 Elections in Jordan," *Middle East Policy*, Vol. XI, No. 2, Summer 2004, pp. 138–151.

Sachs, Jeffrey D., and Andrew M. Warner, "The Big Push, Natural Resource Booms and Growth," *Journal of Development Economics*, Vol. 59, No. 1, June 1999, pp. 43–76.

Sageman, Marc, *Understanding Terror Networks*, Philadelphia, Pa.: University of Pennsylvania Press, 2004.

Saghir, Jamal, "Strategic Provision of Water Sector Services in MENA," presentation, Mediterranean Development Forum, Washington, D.C., March 6–8, 2000.

Sakr, Naomi, *Satellite Realms: Transnational Television, Globalization and the Middle East*, London: I. B. Tauris, 2001.

"Saudi Scraps Wheat Growing to Save Water," *Middle East Online*, January 8, 2008.

Saxena, Prem C., Andrzej Kulczycki, and Rozzet Jurdi, "Nuptiality Transition and Marriage Squeeze in Lebanon: Consequences of Sixteen Years of Civil War," *Journal of Comparative Marriage Studies*, Vol. 35, Spring 2004.

Scham, Paul L., and Russell E. Lucas, "'Normalization' and 'Anti-Normalization' in Jordan: The Public Debate," *Middle East Review of International Affairs*, Vol. 5, No. 3, September 2001. As of October 2, 2010:
http://meria.idc.ac.il/journal/2001/issue3/jv5n3a5.html

Schbley, Ayla, "Religious Terrorism, the Media, and International Islamization Terrorism: Justifying the Unjustifiable," *Studies in Conflict and Terrorism*, Vol. 27, No. 3, May 2004, pp. 207–233.

Seib, M., ed., *Media and Conflict in the Twenty-First Century*, New York: Palgrave Macmillan, 2005.

Seib, Philip, "The News Media and the 'Clash of Civilizations,'" *Parameters*, Winter 2004–2005, pp. 71–85. As of October 2, 2010:
http://www.carlisle.army.mil/USAWC/parameters/Articles/04winter/seib.htm

Shah, Nasra M., "Women's Socioeconomic Characteristics and Marital Patterns in a Rapidly Developing Muslim Society, Kuwait," *Journal of Comparative Family Studies*, Vol. 35, Spring 2004.

Sharp, Jeremy M., *The Al-Jazeera News Network: Opportunity or Challenge for U.S. Foreign Policy in the Middle East?* Washington, D.C.: Congressional Research Service, report for Congress RL31889, July 23, 2003.

Sharp, Jeremy, "The Middle East Television Network: An Overview," CRS Report for Congress, February 9, 2005.

Sheffer, Gabriel, "Ethno-National Diasporas and Security," *Survival*, Vol. 36, No. 1, Spring 1994, pp. 60–79.

Sheikhani, Shirzad, "Iraqi Kurdish Satellite Channels: From Media Obscurity to the Dream of International Broadcasting," *Asharq Al-Awsat*, No. 9068, September 26, 2003, p. 13.

Sivan, Emmanuel, "Illusions of Change," *Journal of Democracy*, Vol. 11, No. 3, July 2000, pp. 69–83.

———, "The Clash Within Islam," *Survival*, Vol. 45, No. 1, January 2003, pp. 25–44.

Sobelman, Daniel, *New Rules of the Game: Israel and Hizbollah After the Withdrawal from Lebanon*, Tel Aviv: Jaffe Center for Strategic Studies, memorandum 69, January 2004.

Stalinsky, Steven, "Inside the Saudi Classroom," *National Review*, February 7, 2003. As of October 2, 2010:
http://www.nationalreview.com/articles/205833/inside-saudi-classroom/steven-stalinsky

Swamy, Anand V., Stephen Knack, Young Lee, and Omar Azfar, "Gender and Corruption," *Journal of Development Economics*, Vol. 64, No. 1, 2001, pp. 25–55.

Tehranian, Majid, "Disenchanted Worlds: Secularization and Democratization in the Middle East," in Amin Saikal and Albrecht Schnabel, eds., *Democratization in the Middle East: Experiences, Struggles, Challenges*, Tokyo: United Nations University Press, 2003, pp. 79–102.

Teitelbaum, Joshua, "Dueling for Da'wa: State vs. Society on the Saudi Internet," *Middle East Journal*, Vol. 56, No. 2, 2002, pp. 222–239.

Telhami, Shibley, *Anwar Sadat Chair for Peace and Development University of Maryland/Zogby International 2006 Annual Arab Public Opinion Survey: A Six Country Study—Egypt, Jordan, Lebanon, Morocco, Saudi Arabia (KSA) and UAE*, Washington, D.C.: Saban Center for Middle East Policy at the Brookings Institution, February 8, 2007a. As of October 2, 2010:
http://www.brookings.edu/views/speeches/telhami20070208.pdf

———, "In the Shadow of the Iraq War: America in Arab Eyes," *Survival*, Vol. 49, No. 1, Spring 2007b. As of October 2, 2010:
http://www.brookings.edu/articles/2007/spring_islamicworld_telhami.aspx

Thaler, David E., Theodore W. Karasik, Dalia Dassa Kaye, Jennifer D. P. Moroney, Frederic Wehrey, Obaid Younossi, Farhana Ali, and Robert A. Guffey, *Future U.S. Security Relationships with Iraq and Afghanistan: U.S. Air Force Roles*, Santa Monica, Calif.: RAND Corporation, MG-681-AF, 2008. As of February 7, 2011:
http://www.rand.org/pubs/monographs/MG681.html

Tilly, Charles, "Cities and States in Europe: 1000–1800," *Theory and Society*, Vol. 18, No. 5, September 1989, pp. 563–584.

"Top Algerian Terrorist Killed," *People's Daily On-Line*, February 10, 2002.

"Top Islamist Militant 'Killed' in Algeria," *BBC News*, February 9, 2002. As of October 14, 2010:
http://news.bbc.co.uk/2/hi/middle_east/1810839.stm

Tripp, Charles, *A History of Iraq*, Cambridge, UK: Cambridge University Press, 2002.

Tumelty, Paul, "An In-Depth Look at the London Bombers," *Terrorism Monitor*, Vol. 3, No. 15, July 28, 2005. As of October 2, 2010:
http://www.jamestown.org/single/?no_cache=1&tx_ttnews[tt_news]=535

"UAE Population to Grow 6% in 2009," *Emirates Business*, May 19, 2009.

"Ulama Surīa Yahatajūn ila al-Asad ala Qarar bi Waqf al-Qabūl bi al-Maāhid al-Sharia [Syrian Ulama Protest to al-Asad over Decision to Stop the Admissions of the Islamic Law Academies]," *Al-Arabiya.net*, July 3, 2006.

UNHCR—*See* United Nations High Commissioner for Refugees.

United Nations Commodity Trade Statistics Database, *UN Comtrade*, undated website. As of October 14, 2010:
http://comtrade.un.org/

United Nations Department of Economic and Social Affairs, Population Division, *World Urbanization Prospects: The 1999 Revision*, New York, ST/ESA/SER. A/194, 2001.

———, *World Urbanization Prospects: The 2005 Revision*, New York, POP/DB/WUP/Rev. 2005, October 2006. As of October 14, 2010:
http://www.un.org/esa/population/publications/WUP2005/2005WUPHighlights_Final_Report.pdf

United Nations Development Programme, *Arab Human Development Report 2002*, New York: United Nations Development Programme, Regional Bureau for Arab States, 2002.

———, *The Arab Human Development Report 2004: Towards Freedom in the Arab World*, New York: United Nations Development Programme Regional Bureau for Arab States, 2005.

United Nations High Commissioner for Refugees, "Statistics on Displaced Iraqis Around the World," April 1, 2007. As of October 14, 2010:
http://www.unhcr.org/461f7cb92.html

United Nations Secretary-General, *Letter Dated 2005/03/24 from the Secretary-General Addressed to the President of the Security Council*, New York: United Nations, S/2005/203, March 24, 2005. As of October 2, 2010:
http://unispal.un.org/UNISPAL.NSF/0/79CD8AAA858FDD2D85256FD500536047

U.S. Census Bureau, *International Data Base*, Washington, D.C., accessed February 8, 2008.

U.S. Department of State, *Country Reports on Terrorism*, Washington, D.C., 2005. As of October 2, 2010:
http://www.state.gov/s/ct/rls/crt/2005/index.htm

Viviano, Frank, "Kingdom on Edge: Saudi Arabia," *National Geographic*, October 2003. As of October 2, 2010:
http://ngm.nationalgeographic.com/features/world/asia/saudi-arabia/saudi-arabia-text.html

Weber, Max, "Politics as a Vocation," in Max Weber, *From Max Weber: Essays in Sociology*, Hans H. Gerth and C. Wright Mills, trans./eds., New York: Oxford University Press, 1958, pp. 77–128.

Wehrey, Frederic, Dalia Dassa Kaye, Jessica Watkins, Jeffrey Martini, and Robert A. Guffey, *The Iraq Effect: The Middle East After the Iraq War*, Santa Monica, Calif.: RAND Corporation, MG-892-AF, 2010. As of February 7, 2011:
http://www.rand.org/pubs/monographs/MG892.html

Weimann, Gabriel, *www.terror.net: How Modern Terrorism Uses the Internet*, Washington, D.C.: U.S. Institute of Peace, special report 116, March 2004. As of October 1, 2010:
http://purl.access.gpo.gov/GPO/LPS47607

———, *Terror on the Internet: The New Arena, the New Challenges*, Washington, D.C.: U.S. Institute of Peace Press, 2006.

Wiktorowicz, Quintan, *The Management of Islamic Activism: Salafis, the Muslim Brotherhood, and State Power in Jordan*, Albany, N.Y.: State University of New York Press, 2001.

———, ed., *Islamic Activism: A Social Movement Theory Approach*, Bloomington, Ind.: Indiana University Press, 2004.

Wiktorowicz, Quintan, and John Kaltner, "Killing in the Name of Islam: Al-Qaeda's Justification for September 11," *Middle East Policy*, Vol. 10, No. 2, June 2003, pp. 76–92.

World Bank, *Education in the Middle East and North Africa: A Strategy Towards Learning for Development*, Washington, D.C.: World Bank, Human Development, Middle East and North Africa, 1998.

———, *Consumer Food Subsidy Programs in the MENA Region*, Washington, D.C., report 19561-MNA, November 12, 1999.

———, "Memorandum of the International Bank for Reconstruction and Development and the International Financial Corporation to the Executive Directors on a Country Strategy for the Arab Republic of Egypt," Report Number 22163-EGT, Washington, D.C.: World Bank, June 5, 2001.

———, "Middle East and North Africa Face Unprecedented Challenge," Development News Media Center, September 26, 2003.

———, *Unlocking the Employment Potential in the Middle East and North Africa: Toward a New Social Contract*, Washington, D.C., 2004. As of October 14, 2010:
http://www.worldbank.icebox.ingenta.com/content/wb/1385

———, *The Palestinian Economy and the Prospects for Its Recovery: Economic Monitoring Report to the Ad Hoc Liaison Committee*, No. 1, December 2005. As of October 2, 2010:
http://siteresources.worldbank.org/INTWESTBANKGAZA/Data/20751555/EMR.pdf

———, *Global Development Finance 2009: Charting a Global Recovery*, Washington, D.C., 2009.

Wright, Robin, "Two Visions of Reformation," in Larry Jay Diamond, Marc F. Plattner, and Daniel Brumberg, eds., *Islam and Democracy in the Middle East*, Baltimore, Md.: Johns Hopkins University Press, 2003.

Zoepf, Katherine, "Many Christians Flee Iraq with Syria the Haven of Choice," *New York Times*, August 5, 2004.